LORD, CHANGE
MY ATTITUDE

James MacDonald
& Barb Peil

LifeWay Press®
Nashville, Tennessee

Published by LifeWay Press®
© 2008 James MacDonald
Seventh printing 2012

ISBN 978-1-4158-2928-8
Item 005035039

Dewey decimal classification: 152.4
Subject headings: ATTITUDE CHANGE \ CHRISTIAN LIFE \ PERSONALITY CHANGE

To order additional copies of this resource, write to LifeWay Church Resources Customer Service: One LifeWay Plaza, Nashville, TN 37234-0113; fax (615) 251-5933; phone toll free (800) 458-2772; e-mail *orderentry@lifeway.com*; order online at *www.lifeway.com*; or visit the LifeWay Christian Store serving you.

Printed in the United States of America

Leadership and Adult Publishing
LifeWay Christian Resources
One LifeWay Plaza
Nasbville, TN 37234-0175

LORD, CHANGE MY ATTITUDE CONTENTS

ABOUT THE AUTHOR

James MacDonald is the founding and senior pastor of Harvest Bible Chapel in the northwestern suburbs of Chicago, Illinois. Harvest Bible Chapel is a church based on prayer, boldness in evangelism, Spirit-filled worship, and unapologetic proclamation of God's Word. In its first two decades, Harvest has grown to more than 12,000. Additionally, it has sent out more than 1,000 leaders to launch 15 new churches with more than 8,000 in attendance.

James's teaching can be heard on the daily, 30-minute radio program *Walk in the Word*, which airs across North America. The mission of *Walk in the Word* is to ignite passion in God's people through the proclamation of truth.

Born in London, Ontario, Canada, James received his master's degree from Trinity Evangelical Divinity School in Deerfield, Illinois, and his doctorate from Phoenix Seminary. He and his wife, Kathy, have three children—Luke, Landon, and Abigail—and reside in Chicago.

For more information about Dr. MacDonald and these ministries, visit *www.harvestbible.org* or *www.walkintheword.com*.

Other Books by James MacDonald
Downpour: He Will Come to Us like the Rain curriculum (LifeWay Press, 2006)
Downpour: He Will Come to Us like the Rain (B&H Publishing Group, 2006)
Ancient Wisdom (B&H Publishing Group, 2006)
Gripped by the Greatness of God curriculum (LifeWay Press, 2005)
Gripped by the Greatness of God (Moody Publishers, 2005)
God Wrote a Book (Crossway Books, 2002)
Seven Words to Change Your Family (Moody Publishers, 2001)
Lord, Change My Attitude … Before It's Too Late (Moody Publishers, 2001)
I Really Want to Change … So, Help Me God (Moody Publishers, 2000)

Barb Peil is the communications director for James MacDonald's radio ministry *Walk in the Word*.

REPLACE A COMPLAINING ATTITUDE ...

When you get out of bed in the morning, what is your attitude? Is it a good indicator of your attitude for the day? Your outlook on life? Find one or two more people with a morning attitude like yours. Talk about whether it's time to change your attitude.

1. Look at the contents page of this book. You'll see five negative and five positive attitudes. Think about the 5–10 people who are closest to you. Which of the attitudes do you see most often? Which do you seldom see? Do you see more negative or positive attitudes?

2. Without reading any content, which one negative and one positive attitude do you most want to read about at this point? Why?

3. Do you think people are aware of or think about their attitudes? How do you think people develop positive or negative attitudes?

4. Do you think it is easy or difficult to change an attitude?

Discussion Questions

25-28
Number 14:26 -30 a 30-31-33
Number 13: 1-24 ; 33 *28*
They suffered because of

Video

In this introductory video, you'll get some general information about what attitudes are and how you can change them. You'll also look at what a complaining attitude does in your life, your relationships, and your witness.

Video Notes

Attitude controls *outcome*.

Those who choose *murmuring* as their lifestyle will spend their lifetime in the *wilderness*.

I Cor. 10:1-3, 6, 9, 11
We choose our *attitudes*.

An attitude is a pattern of *thinking* formed over a long period of time.

Complaining is *sin*. (Hurts God)

__Sin__ means missing the mark.

Complaining means "to express __dissatisfaction__ with a circumstance which is not wrong and about which I am doing nothing myself to correct."

God hears our __complaints__. Num. 11:1

God __hates__ our complaining. (God's heart is hurt when we complain)

God __judges__ our complaining. Psalms 7:11

Wilderness Attitudes

1. Complaining - Number 11:1-3

   If you complain about it and not doing nothing about it, is a sin.

Complaining is a problem.

   Ex. 14:12 15:24 16:3 17:3

God does not want His children complaining about their lot in life.

Psalm 105

Hebrew 12:6; 13:8

Number 11;10;33 12:9 25:4 32:14

1. Am I a complainer.

*2. Am I reaping the consequences of my relationship with God?

3. Am I willing to repent?

Memory Verse

"Do all things without grumbling or questioning,
that you may be blameless and innocent, children of God
without blemish in the midst of a crooked and twisted
generation, among whom you shine as lights in the world."
Philippians 2:14-15

If you have ever traveled the landscape of the Old Testament, you know that it's not all sunny walks in meadows of God's grace. In fact, there are some pretty dark places that I would call deep valleys of mystery where we ask, "God, what are You doing?" We believe that all Scripture is given by inspiration of God so we embrace the entire message of Scripture. The passage we're going to study this week has mystery, but we embrace it as God's revealing Himself to us.

This week we're going to travel to a day when God revealed His heart in an action so radical that it staggers the mind. Think back to when God rescued His people out of Egypt. He raised up a man named Moses to lead them out. Then He parted the Red Sea in a phenomenal act of grace and protection. God assured His people, "I'm going to be a personal God to you. I'm going to lead you to a land flowing with milk and honey. I'm going to bless you, take care of you, and provide for you. It's not going to be easy along the way, but I'm going to be with you." And God delivered on that awesome promise day after day.

You'd think the people would be amazed. They'd been rescued, protected, miraculously fed, clothed, and assured of God's presence by a cloud by day and a pillar of fire at night. You'd think the topic around the campfire every night would be "what awesome thing God did today," or at the least they'd say thanks in their evening prayers.

Instead they griped about what they left behind in Egypt. They fussed about the miracle bread God daily provided. They whined about their future. The complaining escalated to the point that when they got right smack to the edge of the promised land, God said, "Enough!" He was so fed up with their rotten attitudes that He said to Moses, "I'm going to kill them all and start over a new nation with you!" But Moses said, "Lord, don't do that. How would that reflect on You?" So God relented, "All right then. They're going back into the wilderness, and they're going to stay in the wilderness until every single one of them over 20 years old dies. Then I'll give their kids what they wouldn't let Me give to them."

God sent a message: "For every day you shall bear your guilt a year, even forty years" (Num. 14:34, NASB). Forty years for the 40 days of their faithless, grumbling, complaining attitude. God was serious about their complaining attitude!

In spite of all God did for them, the people responded by complaining. The Bible repeatedly refers to their complaining—in the Psalms, in the Prophets, in the Gospels, in the Epistles, and three separate times in the Book of Hebrews. Those who wrote Scripture were always thinking about how radical God feels about grumbling. He hates the doubtful, complaining, rebellious attitude; and He simply won't tolerate it.

If we choose complaining as our lifestyle, we can be absolutely sure that we will be sent to live in the wilderness. The goal of this week's study is to be open to God as He shows us our complaining attitude and invite Him to change us. Let's find out how to stay out of the desert.

I laugh when I think of a wonderful woman in our church who tells this complainer's story. She had made a new meatloaf recipe for her family's dinner. From the moment she set the dish on the table, they had nothing good to say about it. What's this? Ooh, it smells funny. What are those things on the top? Why didn't you make it the old way? Do I have to eat it? Having reached her limit, she picked up the meatloaf without a word, opened the patio door, and chucked the meatloaf—dish and all—over the back fence. She now fears this will be the story that is told at her funeral, the day Mom launched the meatloaf into space.

> *In the short term, complaining separates us from God; in the long term it becomes a lifestyle that sends us to the wilderness.*

Have you ever felt like the mom in this true story? What would you have done in this situation? What would you have wanted to do?

What Do You Think About Complaining?

- [✓] Agree [ ] Disagree 1. Complaining drains your energy and affects your outlook on life.
- [ ] Agree [✓] Disagree 2. Complaining moves you forward in decisive decision-making.
- [✓] Agree [ ] Disagree 3. It's easier to complain than to decide what to do and then do it.
- [ ] Agree [✓] Disagree 4. Complaining is a good way to let your dissatisfaction be heard.
- [✓] Agree [ ] Disagree 5. Complaining feels good.
- [✓] Agree [ ] Disagree 6. Complaining is a way of avoiding taking action.
- [ ] Agree [✓] Disagree 7. Sometimes a situation merits complaints.
- [✓] Agree [ ] Disagree 8. Complaining keeps you from doing anything positive.
- [✓] Agree [ ] Disagree 9. I only complain to help someone understand my perspective.
- [✓] Agree [ ] Disagree 10. I complain more when I feel _stressed + overwhelmed_.
- [✓] Agree [ ] Disagree 11. I complain less when I feel _relaxed and in a structured environment_.

According to our definition, determine if the following actions should be considered complaining. Explain why or why not.

- [ ] Yes [✓] No 1. Asking your small-group leader if the group could consistently dismiss on time since your babysitter needs to be home by a designated hour.

- [✓] Yes [ ] No 2. Asking your spouse what he or she does all day, why the house isn't picked up or why the chores didn't get done over the weekend.

- [✓] Yes [ ] No 3. Sulking because you don't like the way your friend is behaving but when your friend asks you what is wrong, you respond with "nothing."

> *Complaining is to express dissatisfaction with a circumstance which is not wrong and about which I'm not doing anything to correct.*

○ Yes ☑ No 4. Asking the waiter to cook your steak a little more because it is rare and you asked for well done.

☑ Yes ○ No 5. Telling your friends and family how you hate this restaurant because they never cook the food the way you like it.

Is Complaining a Sin?

The word sin means "missing the mark, failing in regard to God's holy standard and just demands." Is complaining a sin? You may be like, "Dude, I don't think so. It may not be a great thing, but a sin? Stealing and lying and blasphemy—sure, they're sins, but complaining? I mean, who am I hurting when I complain?"

Good question. Let's look more closely at the toxic fallout from complaining.

1. You hurt yourself. When you focus on things that bring you down, you nurture a negative perspective on life. This isn't just a violation of the Positive Thinkers Club rules; this is a warning. Remember, when God says, "Don't," He means, "Don't hurt yourself."

Read Philippians 4:8. Instead of complaining, what does God say to think about?

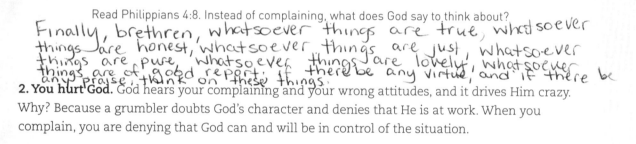

Finally, brethren, whatsoever things are true, whatsoever things are honest, whatsoever things are just, whatsoever things are pure, whatsoever things are lovely, whatsoever things are of good report; if there be any virtue, and if there be any praise, think on these things.

2. You hurt God. God hears your complaining and your wrong attitudes, and it drives Him crazy. Why? Because a grumbler doubts God's character and denies that He is at work. When you complain, you are denying that God can and will be in control of the situation.

What have you complained about that now upon closer evaluation you see that your lack of faith was the real reason for your negative attitude?

3. You hurt the people around you. Like breathing out toxic air, your griping poisons the people around you. Few people keep their complaints to themselves. When you stir things up, you surface new and negative thoughts in the minds of everyone within earshot. They might be working hard to keep a good perspective, and there you go, dumping your cesspool on their territory. We've all been victims of this crime. Recall a time when someone else's attitude poisoned yours. What was the issue? How did your thinking change? If you need help remembering a situation, focus your memory on conversations with people from church. This is Satan's primary target. Get the people murmuring about the music or the carpet color or the pastor's wife, and they won't hear what they desperately need to hear from God's Word.

How have you or can you overcome this kind of destructive attitude pattern? How can you keep it from spreading?

Ask any parent, teacher, small group leader, or pastor what kind of effect complaining has. What do you think is the primary result of a bunch of fussing, whining, complaining people?

The leader feels _____.
The mission is _____.
The group responds by _____.
Who wins? _____

No doubt about it, complaining is a sin. By complaining about your difficult circumstances, you are forfeiting the grace that could help you through it. All the grace and strength you need to experience joy and victory are available to you; but by choosing to complain, by clinging to the idol of a perfect life, you are flushing away the grace of God.

Lord, help me to recognize complaining when I hear it. Soften my heart to what this complaining means to You and to others. Protect me from being poisoned by others' words and by my own attitude. Lord, change my attitude toward complaining. Help me to do it less, love it less, tolerate it less. Forgive me for forgetting Your faithfulness to me. You have given me __a heart of gratitude__ *. Stir faith in me to trust You in good times and bad. Thank You for the ways You are at work in my heart. Amen.*

Back in the Desert

Look up the following Scriptures that describe how the people of Israel complained in the wilderness. Then answer these questions: What was the circumstance? What did the people do? How did God respond?

Exodus 14:10-15

Exodus 15:22-24

Exodus 16:1-7

Exodus 17:1-7

Numbers 11:1

We'll visit the meandering murmurers again tomorrow. For now, consider what God is showing you. Talk to Him right now, asking Him to reveal any new insights into your life about a complaining attitude and what you can do about it.

The atmosphere was dry and hot—scorching even. But the heat wasn't coming from the direction of the wind; it was radiating from inside the campground, in the doorways of the tents—which is like saying "over the back fence"—of the children of Israel. Wilderness attitudes were stirring in the homes of the people who looked longingly in their rearview mirrors at the "good times" they had left behind them in Egypt when they were mistreated as slaves.

The complaining over oppression and bondage that had begun back in Egypt had become convenient carry-on baggage on their flight to freedom. Grumbling had become a way of life. But how could anybody justify complaining in light of the blessings that had been theirs thus far? Could anyone before or since say they have seen God's hand on them with more tangible care and protection? For generations in Egypt, they had lived in the manacles of slavery. Daily they endured the lash on their backs and the paranoid contempt of their Egyptian taskmasters driving them to build another edifice along the Nile. Generations turned under the shadow of suffering at the hands of people who hated them personally and as a race.

Core Passages for Study Today

Exodus 14
Numbers 11
Psalm 106

Then God raised up Moses; and after the ultimate showdown of 10 miraculous plagues that devastated the Egyptians but didn't hurt the Israelites one bit, Pharaoh gave them a "Get Out of Slavery Free" card and welcomed their exodus as every Egyptian home, beginning with his, mourned the sudden, tragic deaths of their firstborn sons. But then Pharaoh, coming to his senses when he called for his dinner and realized his slaves had all left the palace along with his country's entire workforce, rallied his military and raced in hot pursuit after God's people.

How did the newly freed slaves respond? Had the plagues confirmed for them that God could and would take care of them? No. When there appeared to be no escape at the Red Sea, they complained rather than trusting and waiting (Ex. 14:11-12). Complaining not only was their default; it was what kept them slaves, only now to another master.

Sarcasm and Complaining

In Exodus 14:11, the grumblers sarcastically asked Moses, "Is it because there are no graves in Egypt that you have taken us away to die in the wilderness?" How have you used or heard sarcasm used in complaining? Is it effective? Is sarcasm a good vehicle to express dissatisfaction? Why or why not?

Read Exodus 14:11-14.
1. Whom did the complainers turn on?

2. What did they say? Describe their tone of voice as you imagine it to be.

Complaining kept the children of Israel in bondage.

3. What was their attitude prior to the exodus?

4. Why does this surprise/not surprise you?

5. Describe Moses' encouragement to the complainers.

6. What was Moses' wise admonition about what they should do when the Lord fights for them?

What does other Scripture say about our slaves-turned-freemen? Turn to Psalm 106. This historical psalm reveals what was really going on during Israel's wilderness wanderings.

1. According to Psalm 106:7-12, when cornered by their enemy in that desert cul-de-sac, fearful and unable to escape, what had the Israelites forgotten about God?

His wonders and mercies

2. According to verse 8, why did God save them? For His name's sake.

3. According to verse 12, what choice did the Israelites make that combated their fear?

They believed God's word and sang his praises.

True praise affirms God's character. It is more than just positive words; it's a powerful force in battling wilderness attitudes.

Exodus 14:26-30 says that God divided the Red Sea and made a way for them to walk on dry ground "as through a desert" (Ps. 106:9). He led them safely across on dry land. Once on the safe side, they turned and watched that same Red Sea swallow up all of their enemies.

How did the people respond?

Read Exodus 15:1-7. Was the Israelites' song true praise? Explain your answer.

While the tune of Exodus 15:21 still echoed in their heads, not three verses later the people were at it again—complaining, grumbling, forgetful of yesterday's miracles. They were hot, blinded by desert glare, weary, and now thirsty. Exodus 15:24 says, "And the people grumbled against Moses, saying, 'What shall we drink?' "

Read Exodus 15:21-26.
If you could be transported back in time to walk among the people on the evening they camped at Marah, what would you say to the grumblers?

Imagine how they would likely have responded.

Numbers 11:1 says, "And the people complained in the hearing of the Lord about their misfortunes, and when the Lord heard it, his anger was kindled, and the fire of the Lord burned among them and consumed some outlying parts of the camp."

Why was the Lord angry when He heard the people complain?

Speaking God's Language

What love and provision has God made to you?
Psalm 103:2-5

Psalm 116:2

John 14:2-3

2 Corinthians 12:9

Hebrews 13:5

Psalm 106:13-15 continues to describe the events of Numbers 11:4-34.
How did Israel's actions test God?

What was the trade-off for getting what they complained about?

Why is it a risk to demand anything from God?

Just when you think Israel couldn't get any more ungrateful, Psalm 106:19-22 paints an even darker picture. While Moses was away from camp, the Israelites crossed the line. In a matter of weeks, what had started as fearful grumbling at the Red Sea now escalated. Unchecked complaining took them to a new low.

In the following verses from Psalm 106, list the fruit of their complaining:
Verse 20

Verses 21-22

Verse 24

Verse 25

Read Matthew 12:36-37.
What warning do you hear?

What would be different in your manner of conversation if you truly believed what it says?

God Is Faithful Even When We Are Not

God never forgot His promise to Israel. He saw their needs. He heard their cries. He relented from His anger because of His faithful love. But the Israelites wasted their years of wandering. They could have been enjoying a land promised to them that flowed with milk and honey. They could have been living in cities they didn't build and fill houses they didn't furnish, drink water from wells they hadn't dug, and eat fresh fruit from the vine and the orchards they didn't plant. They could have been enjoying blessing after blessing. Instead they chose to complain about what they had given up back in the land of slavery. They chose to live in a wilderness. Like sand through an hourglass, their time to repent, obey, and turn to the Lord was up. God said, "Enough. You want to nurture your wilderness attitude of complaining? Then live in the wilderness the rest of your days."

Psalm 106 records no fewer than five things we do or fail to do that promote a wilderness attitude. Write at least five here with the verse reference.

1.

2.

3.

4.

5.

What have you learned about God's character from Psalm 106? Describe at least three of God's character traits found in this psalm (note verses).

1.

2.

3.

What promise of God are you forfeiting when you choose to complain?

When your murmuring goes unchecked and unrepentant, what blessings do you give up?

Is it worth it? ☐ Yes ☐ No

Start a list today to keep for the rest of this week of situations where you complain, hear complaining, or are tempted to complain. Write down what you were dissatisfied about.

Complaining is not just a habit to kick; it's a perspective to change. Tomorrow, we'll look at where all this fussing comes from.

WEEK 1. DAY 3. FINDING MYSELF IN THE WILDERNESS OF A COMPLAINING ATTITUDE

You might be breathing a sigh of relief that the study hasn't been that convicting. Whew, what was I so worried about? Hang on. We've got some tough wilderness to travel today. But before we go on, let's review. So far in our study we've defined what complaining is and seen a significant example of it in the children of Israel.

We understand that the Israelites had a problem. Now we're going to look at the attitude that comes out of our mouths and heart.

What are your favorite or common complaints?
Check all that have been heard coming out of your mouth.
☐ The amount of work that needs to be done
☐ The weather
☐ Gasoline prices
☐ How your boss is treating you
☐ Never enough money
☐ Incompetent colleagues
☐ Traffic, potholes, trucks, or construction
☐ The music at church
☐ What's on TV/What's not on TV
☐ What the kids are doing/not doing
☐ What your spouse is doing/not doing
☐ Noisy neighbors, noisy children, noisy dogs
☐ An unkempt house
☐ What the pastor or other leader did or said
☐ What the pastor's wife/neighbor/in-law did or said
☐ We never get to ... / We always have to ...
☐ Inept service by unskilled labor
☐ People talking on cell phones while doing something else
☐ Inconvenient requests
☐ Spam in your e-mail and direct marketers on the phone

Did we miss some? Add your own complaints here:

> Are You a Complainer? It's easy to see it in others. It's hard to see it in ourselves. When we complain, we think we're just getting things off our chest. But when other people complain, we're like, "Now that's not helping anything." I challenge you to ask, "God, am I a complainer?"

Profiles in Complaining

It had been one of those days. Another one in a string of bad days when everything had gone wrong. I felt smothered by a blanket of negative feelings. My husband and I argued before we even left the bedroom. My daughter told me that she needed her gym clothes today (news to me). Our neighbor asked if her son could ride to school with us. Does she think I run a taxi service? I tried concentrating on the positives. We have good kids and a solid marriage. We're all healthy. But something had poked a hole in me, and I was being drained by all the "what ifs" in our lives. The list seemed to grow longer every day. Why, God? I grumbled. "Why do we have so many problems? We try to be good Christians. We try to do Your will. When are You going to do something?"

Praying didn't seem to help either. A negative, complaining attitude has become a way of life for me. I'm no fun anymore. Friends stay away. I am my biggest problem. I grumbled about our budget, and it became tighter. I grumbled about my husband's job, and it became more stressful. I grumbled about people in my family, and our relationships became tenser. I can no longer breathe fresh air. So tonight I pray, "God, please forgive me. I'm sure You have grown tired of hearing my whining. Please help me; I don't know how to live any differently anymore."

What Do You Think?

Can you empathize with this woman's struggle? ☐ Yes ☐ No

If yes, in what ways?

Have you ever felt that negative attitudes (like complaining) were smothering you?
☐ Yes ☐ No If yes, how would you describe it?

What was the result of her complaining?

Do you think she'll be OK now that she's prayed about it? Why?

Have you ever felt caught in an endless loop of complaining and problems? ☐ Yes ☐ No
What happened?

How did you get out of it? Are you out of it?

Do you need to stop here and talk to the Lord about a lifestyle choice of negative thinking and complaining that has you trapped and frustrated? Ask His Spirit to show you what you need to see about your life right now. Don't drag this burden around any longer.

Are You a Complainer?

Earlier you listed some things you complain about. Take a look at your list. Does it mostly reflect your home life, your work life, your church life, your personal life, or a combination of these? Identify one thing in each of the following categories that you'd like to see changed.

Does someone living by faith complain?

Home Life	Work Life	Church Life	My Life

Do you complain about these? ☐ Yes ☐ No ☐ I don't think so
Who usually hears your grumbling?

Can you identify a pattern of thinking and complaining that you've nurtured in how you think about this area of your life? (Example: The boss is always unfair.)

What do you say? What are your common comments?

Circle the one you've complained about longest.
Star the one that you complain about most passionately.
Underline the one you complain about most.
Draw a line to the one that you never before thought of as complaining.

Be wise! The strongest muscle in the human body is right behind your teeth. What you say comes right from the heart, pours out through the lips; and before you know it, hearts are broken, relationships are damaged, and a dull gray mist has covered all that God intended to be beautiful in your life. When you have a complaining attitude, the Spirit of God is not in control of your heart so everything that comes out of your mouth is from the human point of view.

Read the following verses from the Bible's wisdom books. Draw principles to confirm in your heart the importance of your words, specifically regarding negative attitudes that come out of your mouth. State your response in the first-person, "When I complain ..." or, "I see now that ..." or, "The best thing for me to do when ..."

Example—Proverbs 10:1: "When words are many, transgression is not lacking, but whoever restrains his lips is prudent."
Your response: I am wise when I restrain/control/limit what comes out of my mouth. I am foolish when I let whatever comes into my head come spewing out of my mouth.

Psalm 141:3: "Set a guard, O Lord, over my mouth; keep watch over the door of my lips!"

Proverbs 10:11: "The mouth of the righteous is a fountain of life, but the mouth of the wicked conceals violence."

Proverbs 14:7: "Leave the presence of a fool, for there you do not meet words of knowledge."

Proverbs 17:27: "Whoever restrains his words has knowledge, and he who has a cool spirit is a man of understanding."

Proverbs 18:2: "A fool takes no pleasure in understanding, but only in expressing his opinion."

Ecclesiastes 10:12: "The words of a wise man's mouth win him favor, but the lips of a fool consume him."

James 1:26: "If anyone thinks he is religious and does not bridle his tongue but deceives his heart, this person's religion is worthless."

It won't be automatic or overnight, but if you stick with it and remain sensitive to what God is teaching you, lasting joy and true "promised land" living is not as far away as you might think.

From Our Mouths to God's Ears
In addition to the comforting truth of Psalm 116:1, "I love the Lord, because he has heard my voice and my pleas for mercy," is the sobering truth that God listens to what I say. He hears my complaining attitude, too, and He hates it! It breaks His heart. It's a slap in His face. It insults His grace. And it makes Him angry.

Why should God take our attitude so personally?

Psalm 7:11, says, "God is a righteous judge, and a God who feels indignation every day." Every day? Even now? God still gets that angry over His people's negative attitude.

What made God angry in ... ?
Numbers 11:1

Numbers 11:10

Numbers 11:33

But isn't God a God of love? Yes, He is. In His infinite transcendence God can both love us and hate our sin at the same time. God can embrace us and forgive us eternally but judge us in the moment because the attitudes of our heart are not pleasing to Him.

What Are You Saying?

Ephesians 4:29 provides a good grid for us to evaluate what should be coming out of our mouths. What three criteria do you see for evaluating what you say?

Before You Complain, Ask Yourself

Is anything corrupt or rotten coming out of your mouth? Evaluate your words carefully.

Are you meeting a need? Someone else's need, that is. When you give voice to a negative attitude, more often it is to get affirmation, sympathy, or advice that fills your cup. Your complaining is totally self-centered rather than other-centered.

Are you benefiting others? To *benefit* means "a kind act; anything contributing to improvement in a condition; advantage; help." Using that definition, do you want what you say to improve rather than impair a situation or someone else's perspective?

If your answers show a complaining attitude, ask God to help you change.

If you're wondering what you can talk about if you stop complaining, here are a few ideas.

Talk about the Lord. Tell others what God has done. Psalm 40:10 states, "I have spoken of your faithfulness and your salvation; I have not concealed your steadfast love and your faithfulness from the great congregation."

Pass on knowledge/instruction. Colossians 3:16 directs us to "let the word of Christ dwell in you richly, teaching and admonishing one another in all wisdom."

Or better yet, learn how to listen. Memorize Proverbs 18:2, NIV, "A fool finds no pleasure in understanding but delights in airing his own opinions."

Before You Make a Formal Complaint

Life is full of imperfections that eat at our peace and prompt us to complain. Next time, before bringing up an issue to an authority, check your attitude. Are you doing good or just stirring the pot?

Words are powerful; take them seriously.

What is your real motive in wanting to complain? Do you want to be noticed? Do you want your own way? Do you want to vent or blame? What does 1 Corinthians 13:4-6 say about motives?

Is there a biblical principle behind this issue? Could it be that this is a matter of personal taste or style rather than an issue to complain about? What does 2 Timothy 2:15 assure us if we apply God's Word correctly?

Is this problem something you should address? Could God want you to pray about this rather than confront it at this time? What insight does John 15:5 give in regard to this decision?

Could you be the problem? Is this irritation God's tool of correction or instruction in your life? Could this situation fall in the "James 1:2-4" category? Take a look in the mirror.

As this issue stirs in your heart, are you being humble? Are you bearing with others in love? How does your life compare with Ephesians 4:1-3? What specifics do you need to remember?

Are you demanding that things be done your way? This could be trouble. Seek the Lord on this. Ask the Lord to give you a submissive heart according to Hebrews 13:17. Before you complain about this issue, what do you need to remember?

Can you state your input in the form of constructive suggestions rather than complaint or criticism? In an effort to apply Colossians 3:12-14, write out the issue as suggestions. Put it away for a few days; then reread them. Edit out any hint of anger. Keep whatever is helpful.

Are you willing to be part of the solution? Back up your words with actions and love. Of what practical reality does Colossians 3:23-24 remind you?

Don't Get Tripped Up

As we run hard after the Lord, our complaining attitude is like a pothole in the road. Too frequently, we fall into it, twist our ankles, and scrape our knees and hands. Left unchecked, this wicked attitude will hurt us every time and perhaps keep us from finishing strong.

Hebrews 12:1, NIV, says that we need to "throw off everything that hinders," and thus avoid some of "the sin that so easily entangles." We've seen today that a negative complaining spirit holds us back. Our negative words are like rocks in our pockets when we're trying to run. Don't rationalize your attitude. Rearranging or renaming the same spirit won't help. You've got to dump the rocks on the side of the road and keep running the race.

How have you seen today that complaining disqualifies you from winning?

Can people say of you, "I've never heard you complain? You just did your job while fixing your eyes on Jesus"?

When I look to see who is guilty of complaining, Lord, I see my own reflection in the mirror. I am so sorry for every careless, caustic, self-promoting word I've said. I see now that this is a serious problem—one that divides the body, destroys the good, and angers You. Open my eyes to see the root of my sin and to confess it to You. Amen.

WEEK 1. DAY 4. FINDING THE ROOT AND PICKING THE FRUIT OF A COMPLAINING ATTITUDE

God never just shrugs off complainers. He deals with them. If you are a chronic complainer, just set your watch: discipline is coming. A time will come when the Lord will say, "That's it!" And you'll learn to hold your tongue. The Lord has 101 ways to help you with that. He never turns His back and says, "Well, you know, that's just the way they are." He will come after you. Complaining isn't just a little problem with attitude; it's a major problem that poisons you and everyone around you. Today we study the root and the fruit of complaining. It's not pretty, nor is it easy; but if we're honest, we can't say we're surprised by any of it.

How God Provided

Review in your mind how God worked to free His people from bondage in Egypt. Time after time He stepped in with a miracle, and yet the Israelites complained.

When they whined to Moses and Aaron, "You have brought us out into this desert to starve this entire assembly to death" (Ex. 16:3, NIV), God heard their complaints and provided manna from heaven. When they grumbled about the lack of water, God provided water from a rock. He protected them from their enemies, gave them His commandments, and filled the tabernacle with His glory. Yet the Israelites continued to complain about their hardships. Then they grumbled about the manna, and God said, "Enough." He sent them meat but accompanied it with a plague (see Num. 11). When they reached the promised land, they again began grumbling out of unbelief. "If only we had died in Egypt! Or in this desert! Why is the Lord bringing us to this land only to let us fall by the sword? Our wives and children will be taken as plunder. Wouldn't it be better for us to go back to Egypt?" (Num. 14:2-3, NIV).

Why Do People Complain?
- ☐ They have a lot of problems.
- ☐ They feel helpless.
- ☐ They'd rather talk about a problem than solve it.
- ☐ They've lost heart.
- ☐ They don't think there's a solution.

The Lord heard their grumbling. He instructed Moses and Aaron to tell them, "As surely as I live, declares the Lord, I will do to you the very things I heard you say: In this desert your bodies will fall—every one of you twenty years old or more who was counted in the census and who has grumbled against me. Not one of you will enter the land. ... As for your children that you said would be taken as plunder, I will bring them in to enjoy the land you have rejected" (Num. 14:28-31, NIV).

Moses wanted those people to see the God he had seen in that burning bush and to trust the cloud that moved unerringly toward the land promised them, but they didn't. He wanted them to love the manna and to have a heavenly appetite that enjoys a heavenly food, but they didn't. He wanted them to be amazed at how God protected them and grateful for His attention and for hearing them all those years, but they didn't. The more they complained, the worse things got.

> Is your memory as short as theirs? As soon as everything wasn't going the way or as fast as they wanted it, they began to doubt and grumble. Are you like that? What amazing acts of God in your life are you forgetting?

Are you reaping the consequences in your relationship with God? Do you wonder why life is a wilderness right now? Could a negative, complaining attitude be the problem? If God could whisper into your heart right now, "I'm listening. I hear everything you say. I hear every thought you think—all of it. You'll never know my joy if you keep that up." If your life lacks a sense of God's favor and presence, ask yourself, "Could it be my attitude?"

Be Careful What You Demand

The Israelites complained about manna and demanded meat, and the Lord told them He would give them meat to eat. The Lord said, "You shall not eat just one day ... but a whole month, until it comes out at your nostrils and becomes loathsome to you, because you have rejected the Lord who is among you and have wept before him, saying, 'Why did we come out of Egypt?' " (Num. 11:19-20). The Lord, knowing their hearts, knew they'd rejected Him for their appetites. So He gave them what they thought they wanted.

God sent a wind to bring quail in from the sea, and they covered the ground three feet deep for a day's walk in any direction. The scene must have been like a riot: people screaming, birds flapping their wings, everywhere the chaotic movement of a meat-hungry people in a sea of birds. The birds were everywhere, pecking and squawking. And while they were chewing the quail, "the Lord struck the people with a very severe plague" (Num 11:33, NASB), and they died by the hundreds. Instead of dancing, they mourned. Instead of grace, they now grieved. And all who had been greedy died and were buried. So they named this cemetery place, kibrothhattaavah, "the graves of gluttony" (Num 11:34, NLT).

Agree or Disagree? Complaining amplifies frustration, spreads discontent and discord, and can invoke an invitation for the destroyer to cause havoc with our lives.

Questions to Ponder

• Are you restless in your faith because you haven't seen an answer to some important prayer?
• Have you been grumbling because you've trusted God for a need you feel He hasn't met?
• Have you been ungrateful for what the Lord has given you?

Don't allow your flesh to win. Reflect on these questions here.

Psalm 106:15 (KJV) says, "[God] gave them their request; but sent leanness into their soul."

They Listened to Others Who Were Complaining.

"The rabble who were among them had greedy desires" (Num. 11:4, NASB). God's people were listening to "the rabble." When they left Egypt, some among them were not Jews. Theirs was a mixed multitude. The Gentiles who didn't know the Israelites' God were mixed in with the Hebrews who did. Naturally you can expect different attitudes. The Israelites chose to listen to those who didn't walk by faith.

Question: Who stirs up your lack of faith? Those who don't know the Lord? Those who have never tasted His goodness? who haven't received the pardon of heaven and the forgiveness of sin? Do you sometimes listen to these people when it's hard to trust God?

Reflect on a time when you let someone outside the faith influence your attitude.

They Focused on What They Didn't Have

"We are up to here with manna." Never mind that they were free. Never mind that they were saved from their enemies in dramatic, awesome ways. Never mind that they had a visual reminder by day and by night that God was with them. Never mind that their leader talked with God on a regular basis. Never mind that their shoes and their clothes never wore out. Never mind all of that. They were just sick of the food. They focused on what they didn't have. They were not grateful for what God provided. He gave manna—"angel's food" is what the psalmist calls it (Ps. 78:25). But they didn't want it; they were used to Egyptian food.

The parallel is painfully close to home. Do you start to complain when you focus on what you don't have rather than trusting God to provide what you need? When you forget all that you've received from God's hand, it happens every time.

Reflect here on the blessings you've received from God lately.

Draw a pattern of thinking that could develop over time if complaining is not stopped. Put these words/concepts in an order that will naturally follow when complaining is allowed to go unchecked. Be ready to explain your thinking in why this order will occur.

Dissatisfaction	Disobedience	Lack of Faith	Skepticism Grumbling
Bitterness	Resentment	Rebellion	Criticizing Leadership
Cynicism	Doubting God		

_____ leads to _____ leads to _____ leads to

_____ leads to _____ leads to _____ leads to

_____ leads to _____ leads to _____ leads to

_____ leads to _____ and this leads far away from God.

Three Common Complaints

The Israelite's wilderness journey exposes the root of their complaints—some serious attitude sins! These three complaints get us into trouble every time. Be honest and see if you find yourself in these accounts in Numbers.

1. Complaints of the Flesh

Numbers 11 makes even the strongest leaders weep when they get a clear picture of what God and Moses had to put up with while trying to lead the people out of Egypt into the promised land. "Now the people complained about their hardships in the hearing of the Lord" (v. 1, NIV). What was the root of their complaint? Food! They craved food other than what the Lord was providing. They wailed, "If only we had meat to eat! We remember the fish we ate in Egypt at no cost—also the cucumbers, melons, leeks, onions and garlic. But now we have lost our appetite. We never see anything but this manna!" (vv. 4-6, NIV).

They completely lost their direction. They forgot that they were eating food they didn't work for, pay for, or do anything to get except to pick it up. But they whined, "We don't want it; we want Egypt!" They let the things they taste, touch, smell, and feel dictate the priorities of their lives.

It sounds foolish to us to hear that they made all that stink over food, but what fleshly pursuit or entitlement has been the subject of your complaints?

2. Complaints of Jealousy

Another dangerous complaint that's buried in each one of us like a ticking bomb is unearthed in Numbers 12:1. "Then Miriam and Aaron spoke against Moses because of the Cushite woman whom he had married" (v. 1, NASB). On the surface their complaint seemed to be about Moses' choice of a wife, but a few verses later their real complaint came out. In the next verse they said, "Has the Lord spoken only through Moses? Has He not spoken through us as well?" (v. 2, NASB). God put Moses in charge and demanded he be respected, and Moses' own brother and sister couldn't stand it! Their complaint didn't come from physical appetite; they complained because of pride!

Are you complaining because no one recognizes your gifts? Are you picking at the flaws in leaders? Are you murmuring because someone besides you is getting attention and praise?
☐ Yes ☐ No ☐ Sometimes

3. Complaints of Authority

In Numbers 13, we find that the complaints against Moses and Aaron have really heated up. What's key for us is the way they handled it.

At the Lord's command Moses chose 12 men to spy out the land of Canaan. He sent the best men from each of the tribes. Joshua and Caleb led them across the Jordan to establish a strategy, but they returned with two different reports. Caleb was full of faith. He said, "We should by all means go up and take possession of it, for we shall surely overcome it" (v. 30, NASB). But the other men gave out to the sons of Israel a bad report ... saying, 'The land ... devours its inhabitants; and all the people whom we saw in it are men of great size' " (v. 32, NASB). They totally lost sight of God.

They spent all night complaining against Moses and Aaron. Their plan was to kill them, appoint a new leader, and return to Egypt. Did they think God would open the Red Sea for them again? Or that the Egyptians would be happy to see them after they had drowned their whole army? What began as a lack of confidence in themselves led to lack of confidence in their leader and ended with a complete lack of faith in God

Complaining is addictive. The cycle goes like this: You've got a problem. You complain and get stuck in the problem. The enemy of your soul takes advantage and causes you to complain more. You live in constant crisis.

Complaining Is Destructive

God sees our complaining as an insult to His provision. When the Israelites did it, He destroyed them. "[Do not] grumble, as some of them did and were destroyed by the Destroyer. Now these things happened to them as an example, but they were written for our instruction" (1 Cor. 10:10-11). Take the warning.

Complaining Can Make You Sick

Solomon said, "A calm and undisturbed mind and heart are the health of the body" (Prov. 14:30, AMP). How many "calm and undisturbed" complainers do you know?

"Now when the people complained, it displeased the Lord" (Num. 11:1, NKJV). As we've looked at how God dealt with the Israelites, we understand that He takes complaining personally. He considers our grousing an act of unbelief directed toward Him. He's the One who provides us life and breath, health and security, food and drink; yet when we complain, we're saying that His provision isn't good enough. What have You done for me lately, God? And why haven't You done this for me? Our complaints are insults, verbalizing that we don't trust Him to provide, protect, and order our lives. To the Lord complaining feels like an accusation that He's not taking care of us.

Do you see His point? ☐ Yes ☐ No
Why?

Knowing that God takes complaining this way, how do you feel about your negative attitudes?

The root of complaining is unbelief. "And we know that for those who love God all things work together for good, for those who are called according to his purpose" (Rom. 8:28).

What is needed for someone who is trapped in a habit of complaining to receive the truth of Romans 8:28?

Paul warned Christians to avoid the danger of complaining. "Nor grumble, as some of them did and were destroyed by the Destroyer" (1 Cor. 10:10). Complaining opens the door to Satan's destructive strategies. Our whining alerts the predator that a victim is in the neighborhood.

How could Satan use our complaining for his purposes?

Have you seen this in your life?

How does complaining run counter to Ephesians 4:12-15 and Colossians 1:18?

"Then they despised the pleasant land, having no faith in his promise. They murmured in their tents, and did not obey the voice of the Lord" (Ps. 106:24-25).

Lord, will You perform radical surgery in my heart and show me the vast benefits of a life of faith. Take away my panic and the fear, and replace it with a calm, quiet confidence that You are worthy of every ounce of my trust. You are more worthy than I can begin to understand. Convict me of my complaining spirit. Cause me to hate the offense that hurts our relationship. I now see complaining as sin and confess it, turn from it, and run to You. I entrust to You my biggest and hardest struggle right now and wait in faith for You. Amen.

WEEK 1. DAY 5. WRAPPING UP THE WILDERNESS OF A COMPLAINING ATTITUDE

I don't know about you, but I'm so sick of these Israelites who wouldn't trust God. I'm weary of their complaining. I'm frustrated by their inability to see a bigger picture. I'm angry at how they insulted God. No wonder God decided they would all die in the wilderness.

We're all about honesty in our walk with Christ so I have to confess that one reason I'm ready to move on is because their story hits way too close to home. I could have easily been one of those who died in the desert. Oh, you too? Thanks for your honesty. I'd like to think I would have chosen differently. I love the thought of standing with Joshua and Caleb, filled with faith and ready to take the land. But I can't be sure I would have done that. Why? Because I know my heart. God had this distressing account written down and referenced in so many places in the Bible because He knows all our hearts, and He wanted to get this message to us wherever we turned in His Word. "Each of us has turned to his own way," wrote the prophet Isaiah (Isa. 53:6, NASB).

- All of us have been guilty of craving things God doesn't want us to have.
- All of us have been blasé about amazing miracles God does all around us.
- All of us have doubted His power to provide.
- All of us have forgotten "his works and the wonders that He had shown [us]" (Ps. 78:11).
- All of us have refused to believe at one time or another that He was more than what we imagined He could be.
- We've all complained in some dark moment that God just isn't enough. If we've ever wondered if God will forgive us if we turn in repentance, this is the moment to believe. We've spent four focused days looking at the children of Israel, looking at ourselves, and looking at the Lord.

We've learned:
Day 1. What complaining is and what it is not.
Day 2. What the Israelites did that made God so angry.
Day 3. How to recognize a negative, complaining attitude in your own spirit.
Day 4. The root and fruit of complaining and how it affects your relationship with God.
One last time today let's review the principles and consequences of a negative, complaining attitude so that the Lord can permanently write it on your heart.

> What immediately comes to mind? A Scripture verse? Something you've learned about God? Yourself? Others?

Profiles in Complaining

I was sobered and convicted by the words I read in Numbers 11. The parallel between me and the Israelites was all too clear. God had heard my grumbling when I lost my job 10 months ago. He understood the fear and anxiety behind all my noise and provided for our family in miraculous ways. We didn't starve or even get behind on our bills, yet I was restless and ungrateful. My pride was hurt by this layoff and the realization of how much I needed to trust God.

When I found another job, I continued to grumble even more because it wasn't the perfect job. Instead of praising God for the amazing things He was doing in my wife's spiritual life, I was jealous. The thing she feared (me losing my job) had come true, yet she had never trusted Him more and been more satisfied with Him. I secretly nurtured my bruised ego and even blamed God for the lack of fulfillment of this new position. I know firsthand about the grace of God as Exodus 34:6-7 describes: "The Lord, a God merciful and gracious, slow to anger, and abounding in steadfast love and faithfulness, keeping steadfast love for thousands, forgiving iniquity and transgression and sin, but who will by no means clear the guilty."

God had been gracious to me and slow to anger, but as the story about the Israelites revealed, His patience has a limit. I knew if I continued to grumble I would be in danger of experiencing His punishment. I also knew that whether I acknowledged my complaining as sin, God considered it sin. Left unchecked, grumbling has the power to kill my relationship with God and with other people. It also can cause me to be unfaithful to God, to turn to other sources to find answers to needs that can be met only in Him. "Oh God, help me. I am so sorry. I see my sin, and I'm turning around.

Did this man have a good reason to complain? ☐ Yes ☑ No Why?

Why had he and his wife experienced different spiritual journeys during this time of job change?

Because they experienced this journey with two different attitudes

What attribute of God had the study of Numbers 11 brought to light?

Does this negate God's grace? ☐ Yes ☑ No Complement it? ☐ Yes ☐ No

How did you relate to his honest admissions?

How does fear and discouragement prompt unbelief? What other emotion or mind-set prompts you to complain?

How have you been tempted to turn to sources other than God to find answers to needs that can be met only in Him?

Express Your Satisfaction with God

Read Psalm 13:1-6. Use the outline below to pour your heart out to God.
Step 1. Verbalize your pain (vv. 1-2).

Step 2. Ask for help (vv. 3-4).

Step 3. State your trust in God (v. 5).

Step 4. Commit yourself to praise (v. 6).

Look back over your week's notes. What new insights did you gain?

What understanding of the way God works was refreshed?

How does God want you to respond to what He has shown you?

Write a prayer below expressing your heart to God about this whole matter of negative thinking and disbelief.

Lord, change my complaining attitude ...

Are You Willing to Repent?

Are you willing to turn from your sinful attitude, acknowledge that it is wrong before God, and ask Him to change you? We've been studying the Old Testament in this lesson, but we celebrate the good news of Jesus Christ. He died to provide a way for us to be forgiven and cleansed and have a fresh start in life and in our attitudes. I've personally struggled with complaining over the years, and I'm really thankful for a wife who many times took me aside and said, "Your attitude isn't helping anything; we need to pray about this." And so Kathy and I sat down and prayed, "God, I'm sorry for my attitude. It's wrong. I know it's not pleasing to You. Please forgive me and cleanse me." He is faithful to do that in my life, as He is for you.

Every person reading this has something that's difficult about which they could complain. God wants us to trust Him with that. But when all we do is complain about that thing, whatever it is, we turn away from all the good things He has done. I know it's hard. But hear a pastor's heart. You are forfeiting the grace that could help you through that trial by complaining about it instead of embracing it as a tool used by God to keep you humble and keep you close to Him. You say, "But I was close to Him." He wants you closer. I am not making light of how hard it is. I'm trying, as lovingly as I know how, to draw the connection between the wilderness existence you're now experiencing and the attitude of resenting that point of adversity in your life. God hears our complaining about a specific combination of circumstances that might be stretching us or about something that God has allowed to keep us close and humble, but He will not tolerate our complaining about it repeatedly.

Instead of stiff-arming God with your complaints, see this as the best opportunity you have to draw near to Him.

By God's Grace I'm Changing!	I Would Normally Murmur	I Will Now Say
When I hear that someone else in my office will represent us at a conference that I was hoping to attend ...		
When my flight is delayed (for the third time), I approach the ticket counter and say ...		
When the other car pool mom calls and says that her entire family is down with the flu and she won't be driving tomorrow, I say ...		
When my wife tells me that my blue suit is still at the cleaners, I ...		
When my husband announces the possibility of a job change and a move to a new city, I ...		
When a fairly new believer in my small group calls to tell me about a need but it escalates more into a gripe session, I ...		

Getting free from a lifelong pattern of grumbling isn't easy. It takes faith and courage as well as a conscious effort not to slip back into old habits. Train yourself to listen for that whine in your voice, to repent immediately, and to turn your grumbles into praise. In next week's lesson learn how to replace your complaining attitude with a thankful attitude.

WITH A THANKFUL ATTITUDE

With a partner or in a group of three, share how your study this week has affected your complaining. Have you noticed when you complain? Give an example of how you have tried to change your complaining response this week.

Discussion Questions
About Complaining

1. What is complaining?

2. What does complaining sound like?

3. Are you a complainer?

4. What is the root and fruit of your complaining?

5. How do you want to change?

Video

Watch and listen for how you can change your attitude from complaining to becoming thankful.

Video Notes

Gratitude is the attitude that sets the altitude for living.

Attitude is _everything_.

God despises a _negative_, fault-finding, faithless attitude. Numbers 14

* _Faith_ grows in the soil of gratitude. (only acknowledging God

Romans 1:18, 20-21

Gratitude—To show that a _Kindness_ received is valued.

Gratitude is the attitude

Psalm 107: 8, 15, 21, 31

Thankfulness is a _decision_. The choice is ours. (I have the comp

Thankfulness is a decision based in _reality._

Thankfulness is a _life_-_changing_ decision.

Replacing a complaining attitude w/ a
thankful^ness attitude

Luke 17   Everyone needs the Lord.
   11-14
   Only a few thank Him personally
   Only a few experience Him powerfully.

Ecclesiastes 3:11
Rom 1:20-21a

1. Am I thankful
   person?

2. Hebrews 13:15
2. 1 Thessalonians
   Ephesians 5:18-20

1. Why should Christians be thankful?

2. To whom should we be thankful?

3. For what should we be thankful?

4. How does being thankful rather than complaining
   make you feel?

5. How does being thankful instead of complaining
   affect your relationship with God?

6. How does being thankful instead of complaining
   affect your relationships with other people?

Discussion Questions
About a Thankful Attitude

Study Challenge

Can you grow in having a thankful attitude? This week's study will take
a look at relevant Scripture passages and help you apply biblical truths
to your life to see if you have a thankful attitude.

Memory Verse
"Give thanks in all circumstances; for this is the will of God in Christ Jesus for you."
1 Thessalonians 5:18

Life is all about choices. Attitude is the first one. When you encounter a situation that is not what you think it should be, you must choose to see it like the proverbial glass half full or the glass half empty. Those two paths take you to different places depending on your attitude.

Week 1 pointed out how strongly God feels about your choice of attitude. In Numbers 14 He said to a whole generation of His own children, "I can't take your attitude anymore. Go on back into the wilderness and die." He loved these people; He miraculously and dramatically rescued them. But no matter what He did for them, they refused to stop murmuring. So God decided to give their kids the blessing they wouldn't let Him give to them—all because they refused to change their attitude. All it would have taken was a heartfelt thank-you. God would have been pleased if they had just been grateful for all the ways He had protected and cared for them just as He had promised to do. A simple acknowledgement of what they had received from His hand is all He wanted. Their gratitude would have changed history.

> Gratitude—To show that a kindness received is valued and appreciated.

You can pick up any self-improvement book or listen to a television talk show that gives a list to a better life, and you'll find that the number one answer is "to be thankful for all the good in your life." Even pagans see the truth in the choice of a thankful attitude. A God-centered, faith-oriented, grateful life is a healthier, happier life. This advice is from people who don't even know God. It's commonly accepted that fulfillment comes when we get outside of ourselves. Joy begins to flow when you stop focusing on the glass half empty but instead on the glass half full by giving thanks. God's fullness comes to those who turn from complaining and embrace thankfulness as the focus of their thought life.

> Giving thanks is a choice you make every day.

Where's your attitude taking you today? You may be putting up a good front, but is your heart stuck somewhere between a complaining and a thankful attitude? Need help getting out of a wilderness? Begin the trek out with this thought: God is kind and good to offer us another path, the higher road of a thankful attitude. Let's get on it.

What Do You think?

- [ ] Agree [✓] Disagree   1. You can only really be thankful when you feel like it.
- [✓] Agree [ ] Disagree   2. Gratitude is greatly underrated as a happiness factor.
- [✓] Agree [ ] Disagree   3. Gratitude doesn't come naturally to me.
- [ ] Agree [✓] Disagree   4. It's OK not to say "thank you" as long as you are thankful.
- [ ] Agree [✓] Disagree   5. Why does God need to be thanked? He does what He wants anyway.
- [✓] Agree [ ] Disagree   6. I am more thankful when I feel _happy_.
- [✓] Agree [ ] Disagree   7. I am less thankful when I feel _tried or bad_.

What's Your Altitude?

We've all spent some days under the clouds of pessimism in negative, ungrateful doldrums. I've lived there long enough to know I don't want to waste another moment of my life dwelling there.

Today we'll focus on another kind of living—a life that soars above and refuses to focus on the negative, up where the air is clean and the sun is shining and the future is as bright as the promises of God. If you have ever flown up there, you know that's where you want to live your life.

How do you get there? By replacing a complaining attitude with a thankful attitude. Thankfulness is a decision based in reality. Nothing in this world will help you with this attitude; but by the power of God's Spirit at work in you, you can choose a life of gratitude. You will still see the negative, but you won't focus on it.

Start here and now. List five things you are grateful for at this moment. You don't need to sound spiritual or profound; just write them down:

1. *My family*
2. *My church home*
3. *My salvation*
4. *My health*
5. *My needs being met*

But what if I don't feel thankful? Great question! The answer is, do it anyway. Emotions make a great caboose but a terrible engine. Too often, when emotions drive our choices, they send us up one side of the roller coaster one day and down the other side the next. Emotions are untrustworthy and should not determine your choice of attitude. Are they the first, maybe the most demanding voice you hear? Most likely. But you can chose the higher altitude and in so doing kindle true gratitude to spark into flame.

Some say you can't plan on being grateful because gratitude is a spontaneous response to the awareness of a kindness received, but gratitude can also be lived as a discipline. The discipline of gratitude is the explicit effort to acknowledge that all I am and have is given to me from God as a gift of love and a gift to be celebrated.

Thanksgiving doesn't depend on the way you feel moment by moment, nor is it a polite courtesy. Your urgent duty is to respond in gratitude to all that God has done and is doing for you. To be grateful is to recognize God's hand on everything that touches your life. Every breath you draw is a gift of His love; every moment of existence is a gift of grace, for it brings with it other immense graces from God. Gratitude takes nothing for granted, is never unresponsive, is constantly aware of new wonders, and praises the goodness of God. Those who are grateful know that God is good not by hearsay but by experience.

How do you know from your own experience that God is good? *He is always with me no matter what I go through or experience*

What Does God's Word Say About a Thankful Attitude?

1. Read Psalm 136.
What two attributes of God's character are being praised?

Do you see God's faithfulness to the children of Israel wandering in the desert? ☐ Yes ☐ No
What are some ways listed here that God took care of them?

How are God's great acts as Creator described here?

Why is that reason for thanksgiving?

When did you last praise Him for the sun, moon, and stars?

2. Read Ephesians 5:15-20.
Name some of the Christian's to-do list commanded in these verses:

3. Read Colossians 3:12-17.
How many times does this passage direct us to have a thankful attitude?

In your own words, what is the general tone of this passage?

How is a thankful attitude a natural part of the spirit of this text?

We can't contrive some mechanical technique to force us to be thankful. But we've learned that our attitudes are patterns of thinking formed over a long time based on what we think and do.

Look Inside

Has the Spirit ever convicted you, or is He convicting you now, with your lack of gratitude? If ingratitude is allowed to become a habit, it will weigh you down with the burdens of your life, leading to bitterness, depression, and despair. This is your day to choose to change. By the Spirit's power you can cultivate an atmosphere of gratitude around your life. You have every reason to be grateful. We dishonor God with anything less.

In what area of life do you need to ask God to open your eyes and reveal His goodness to you?

Where do you need faith to see a situation differently? Write it here as a prayer:

An Exercise for this Week

Think back over last week's lesson. In the time since studying about complaining, how often did you hear murmuring come out of your mouth? How should we put an end to this habit of complaining? Replace it with the habit of gratitude.

Try this simple exercise—simple to understand but not to do. Set your watch. Determine for the next 24 hours that you will not complain. Carry around a piece of paper to record every time you complain or when you catch yourself about to complain. We'll return to this tomorrow.

An Exercise for a Lifetime

You say you want to live in the promised land? You're weary of wilderness living and want to know the fullness and the fulfillment that only God can bring? Get in the habit of rehearsing God's goodness to you. Put a stack of 3 x 5 index cards on your nightstand. At the top of each card write, "Today I am thankful for …" Then make a list of numbers 1–5. If you fill out a card every night before you go to bed, something amazing will happen to your attitude.

Write down the big things and the little things. Write something good that happened today. Lay your head down to sleep with that on your mind. Before your feet hit the floor in the morning, determine to thank Him for the day. Read your list before you begin your day. You can do this in a journal as well. Just do it. This little habit will change your life.

Another lifetime ago, 10 men led healthy, happy lives. Just normal lives—married with kids, doing their best to support their families with a job that promised advancement. They had a future. They had dreams.

But that was long ago … Before the illness had eaten away their bodies. Before the numbness had stolen strength from their limbs and feeling from their fingers and toes. Before their faces had grown disfigured beyond recognition. Before their families said good-bye and turned their backs.

Now they were the walking dead, begging for something, anything. One morning, as they approached yet another village to beg, they heard the name of a visiting Teacher. For months His name had spread through the leper colony like a whispered wildfire: Jesus. He heals lepers. He doesn't turn away. His words restore life. There He was, standing at the well not far from them, and He was looking their way! All at once their 10 pitiful, hoarse voices cried in unison: "Jesus! Master! Have pity on us!" With His eyes and with His words He compassionately told them, "Go show yourselves to the priests." That was all. No touch. So with faith and desperation equal to the moment, the 10 turned to Jerusalem and to the priests who were the only ones who could declare them clean. Nothing had changed, but they also had nothing to lose.

Then came the miracle. Somehow, suddenly, completely, unconditionally, they were cleansed. Their skin was as fresh and smooth as a baby's. They were healthy, whole, healed.

Nine healthy men shouted, cheered, and raced down the road like boys dismissed to the playground and never looked back. But one man, a Samaritan, spun around, ran to Jesus, and flung himself at His feet. Tears spilled down his strong, soft cheeks. Trembling, he whispered two words: "Thank you." This story Jesus told definitively answers the questions: Is a thankful attitude such a big deal? Does God really care that much about how thankful people are? The answer is yes!

This Gospel account of the 10 cleansed lepers prompts a range of emotion—first, sorrow at the terrible suffering they must have endured; then complete joy at the thought of the 10 lepers healed, jumping around on whole legs and shouting out from restored vocal chords.

But the obvious question remains. What about their hearts? If you had been one of those healed that day, would you have run with the nine or returned to thank Jesus? Would you have been grateful? What would you have done? Today we'll explore more from this passage and other parts of Scripture focused on the attitude of gratitude.

> Only when we acknowledge God as the gracious provider of general blessings, like life and breath, food and shelter, do we begin to comprehend our need for God in a personal way and begin to express faith in Him.

Read Luke 17:11-19 and answer the following questions:
The lepers called Jesus, "Master." How was their immediate response a clear indication of their sincere use of this title?

What were the lepers asking Jesus to do when they said, "Have mercy on us"? Why would they have asked this?

The lepers were probably surprised by Jesus' instruction to go show the priest since ...

Describe some of the insights this passage gives us about Jesus' character.

Upon his realization of being healed, whom did the leper praise? Describe the scene.

Why do you think it was important to note at this part of the story that this leper was a Samaritan? Based on what you know about Samaritans, why did this add significance to the miracle or to the testimony of Christ in that time and place?

"Your faith has made you well." What do you think Jesus meant by this when He said it to the one grateful leper. Weren't all 10 lepers made well?

What do you think was the purpose of telling this story in Luke?
- ☐ To illustrate Jesus' healing power
- ☐ To illustrate the humility of a Samaritan
- ☐ To illustrate the importance of a grateful heart
- ☐ To illustrate the neglectful nine lepers

Explain your response:

In addition to returning to his family and normal life, how do you think the leper's life changed after he was healed?

Reflect on a time when God did something miraculous in your life. Was it an answer to prayer? Was it a rescue? Was it a provision? If nothing else, remember when you understood your need for a Savior and you turned to Him. Tell God what you remember from that amazing event in your life. Thank Him again.

> Gratitude unlocks the fullness of life. It turns what we have into enough, and more. It turns denial into acceptance, chaos to order, confusion to clarity. It can turn a meal into a feast, a house into a home, a stranger into a friend. Gratitude makes sense of our past, brings peace for today, and creates a vision for tomorrow.
> —Melody Beattie

A Thankful Attitude Is like Christ
Jesus expressed gratitude. What was Jesus expressing thanks for in the following verses?
John 6:1-13 (specifically v. 11)

Luke 22:19

John 11:41

Thankfulness is an element of Christlikeness. When we're thankful, we're modeling the Master.

It is good to give thanks to the Lord. It's therapeutic; it lifts the soul. Begin to thank God and others for the blessings surrounding you. Do you have a lot to be thankful for? The answer clearly is yes!

In ordinary life we hardly realize that we receive a great deal more than we give, and that it is only with gratitude that life becomes rich.
—Dietrich Bonhoeffer

Try composing or choosing a poem or hymn of thanksgiving to God and offer it as your own prayer. Here is a sample prayer from someone who has committed to make thanksgiving the first thing he does every morning. Compose your own in the space below or in your journal.

O Lord and Maker of all things, thank You for this light that now streams through my windows to rouse me to the life of another day.
Thank You for the life that stirs within me.
Thank You for the bright and beautiful world into which I go.
Thank You for earth and sea and sky, for scudding cloud and singing bird.
Thank You for the work You have given me to do.
Thank You for all that You have given me to fill my leisure hours.
Thank You for my friends.
Thank You for music and books and good company and pure pleasures.
To You, who are everlasting mercy, give me a tender heart today toward all those to whom the morning light brings less joy than it brings to me:
Those in whom the pulse of life grows weak,
Those who must lie in bed through all the sunny hours,
The blind, who are shut off from the light of day,
The overworked, who have no joy of leisure,
The unemployed, who have no joy of labor,
The bereaved, whose hearts and homes are desolate;
And grant Your mercy on them all.
"It is good to give thanks to the Lord, to sing praises to your name, O Most High" (Ps. 92:1).

Our lives often are impoverished of genuine gratitude. We have so much, but we've been taught that the way to deal with receiving much is to make plans to get more and more and more. Answer this honestly: The last time you pulled into the church parking lot, ready for the weekend service, were any of these questions at the center of your heart:

What am I going to get today?
Am I going to be encouraged?
Am I going to be strengthened?
Am I going to be taught?
Am I going to like the worship?
Am I going to appreciate the ministry I receive?

All the focus is on your getting something. Isn't that sad? If God never did another thing for you and me, we could spend the rest of our days filling them with heartfelt gratitude like this: "Thank You, God, for this day." "Thank You for life." "Thank You for breath." "Thank You for health." "Thank You for strength." Too often we make the choice to turn from all that we've received to focus on what we still have to have. That's where the threat of complaining comes in and why we feel like we're living in a wilderness.

> You say, "If I had a little more, I should be very satisfied." You make a mistake. If you are not content with what you have, you would not be satisfied if it were doubled.
> —Charles Spurgeon

The way to put off complaining is not to tape your mouth. The way to put off complaining is to fill your life with genuine expressions of gratitude to God. It's all a matter of perspective. It's where we choose to focus. God's fullness comes to those who turn from complaining and embrace thankfulness as the focus of their thought life. We can learn to direct our attention to those things that draw us to God in appreciation for who He is and what He has done. That's what we're about today.

Let's begin by talking with the Lord:

Father, I know that I need a change of heart. I have excused my complaining attitude, rationalized it until I don't even believe it myself, blamed others for my responsibility. Forgive me for thinking my ingratitude is justified. Forgive me for living so long in the spiritual poverty of a life without gratitude, and grant me a renewed and extended season of mercy and grace.

Lord, right now I lift my heart to You in a thankful spirit. I'm letting go of bitterness, resentment toward others—all the things that keep me dry and distant from You. I'm repenting of them. Produce grief in my heart over them. How could I slap away Your hand of generosity? Now I'm turning back to You. Well up in me the sweetness of restoration and the rightness of reconciliation to You. I know that this journey has just begun. Help me to prioritize time to seek You in Your Word and in prayer. Help me to remember the priority of gratitude before I experience it, to express it even before I feel it. Thank You that as I humble myself in Your sight You will lift me up. This I pray in Jesus' name. Amen.

Psalm 138 is a fantastic primer on how to thank God for His grace and mercy toward us. For a few minutes put yourself in the room with David as he wrote this thanksgiving prayer to God and discover five reasons we can thank God. Real gratitude starts deep inside and ripples out to the surface. It is not shallow or frivolous, flippant or superficial. Praise is the deepest expression of the soul in love with God. That's what David was saying: "With all my heart I give You thanks."

That word *thanks* has got an interesting nuance beyond the normal use of the term. It means "to give public acknowledgement." It's the idea of telling others about something that means a lot to us. It's bragging on someone that we love.

It feels like a contamination even to mention the gods of the Canaanites here, but David was living in reality. Even as we live in a dark sinful world, we can worship God.

Why was David singing? Why did he want to brag on God's name? It's personal: "On the day I called, you answered me; my strength of soul you increased" (v. 3). David admitted, "God, I had a need that was so huge. I brought it to You and laid it out before You, and I gave You thanks for whatever You wished to do with my need. You could have done anything, but You chose to answer me. You gave me insight. You gave me relief. You gave me help. I give You praise for being that kind of God and giving me an answer."

Has God answered a specific prayer you've prayed lately? Has God restored a relationship that has been damaged for a long time? Has He given relief from physical pain? Has a child come home and back to God? Has God provided a job? Reflect right now on how God has answered a need in your life.

Our great God is in touch with the lowly. He moves up close to us. He pulls us near. He comforts us when we may feel lonely and rejected. As a fugitive, as a king, as a warrior, David knew what it was like to be on the run for his life. He knew all about rejection and loneliness. David said the second reason we should give thanks is that God gives us hope. When we have every good reason to despair, David reminds us that our God rescues us and gives us hope.

How is God your rescue and hope? Was there ever a time when you were lost but then found? Were you once without hope but now live in expectation? Write your situation here. Brag on what God did for you:

God is working on you. He's elbow deep in your life. His tools are His steadfast (faithful) love. He's staying with you to accomplish what He wants to fulfill in you. God finishes what He starts. He cares more about your becoming more like His Son than you do. "And I am sure of this, that he who began a good work in you will bring it to completion at the day of Jesus Christ" (Phil. 1:6). Isn't that amazing? Reason 3 to give thanks is that God isn't finished working on you. Tell God right now: "Don't stop working on me!" Surrender to His chisel and be thankful He loves you so much He's never going to stop.

The apostle Paul was confronted with the decision to complain or be thankful time after time in the latter years of his life. Paul wrote his letter to Philemon while in prison—falsely accused, falsely condemned for trying to do what's right. He started his letter off with, "I'm thankful" (v. 4). Here's a man who's saying, "I'm not going to let circumstances get me down. I'm not going to let these disappointments and heartaches distract me. I thank God for you." Paul was thankful for the goodness of God, regardless of the circumstances.

As you read the letter to Philemon, note three ways Paul's attitude of gratitude appears here.

1.

2.

3.

Following Paul's model, try it out here. Write your complaint about your hardship on the left and a godly response of gratitude on the right.

Complaint   Thanks

Cultivate the Discipline of Gratitude

Give your attention and care to those whose lives make your particular blessings stand out by comparison. Have you been grumbling that you can't afford a new couch for the living room? Go serve in a soup kitchen for the homeless. Have you found it hard to thank God for your boss? Talk a few minutes with the folks in the unemployment line. Do you complain about minor aches and pains? Pray for someone with a terminal illness. Your gratitude to God is sure to grow.

Complete this chart with thanksgiving for gifts in your life.

Things I'm Glad I Have	People I Appreciate	Spiritual Blessings	Everything Else

Read this list four times in the next 24 hours. After lunch, after dinner, before going to sleep, before beginning work. (Really do this! I'm going to ask you about it on Friday.)

Complaining is not just a habit to kick; it's a perspective to change. Tomorrow we'll look at the source of all this fussing.

Proud people don't say, "Thank you." Proud people never think they get as much as they deserve. To be grateful at all is to see yourself as a benefactor of someone else's grace. Humility, then, is the soil of gratitude.

To be grateful, after all, is to recognize that all of life is a gracious gift from God's hand. It's to see ourselves in proper perspective to God, ourselves, and our world. We are all debtors to God's common blessings, beginning with life and breath and health and strength all the way down to the specific ways He is working in our lives this moment—forgiving us of our latest sin, bearing with us in our growing pains, providing for us in ways that bring us joy, teaching us insight from His Word that nurtures and sustains us in trial, giving us the ability to love and be loved, comforting us with His Spirit's voice, and drawing us into closer fellowship with Him. Gratitude sees it all from God.

As we have learned, ingratitude is a clear indicator of the heart that has turned in on itself—of the proud, restless ego that is never satisfied—on those who believe the world owes them whatever they can get. Whether complaining that the gift is not good enough or too absorbed in the gift to say, "Thank you," those who are not thankful thumb their noses at God in favor of themselves.

If this sounds too harsh, you need to read Romans 1 to see the connection between ingratitude and some of the most tragic depravities of sin. A thankless heart is at the root: "For although they knew God, they did not honor him as God or give thanks to him, but they became futile in their thinking, and their foolish hearts were darkened" (Rom. 1:21).

Those who refuse to thank God for how He has made them and what He has given them walk in darkness, unable to see the light of reality. They've exchanged the truth about His grace for the lie of self-absorption. Paul says the result of ingratitude and people's refusal to acknowledge God is that "God [gives] them up to a debased mind to do what ought not to be done" (v. 28). The list is a range of incredibly dark things—"gossips, slanderers, haters of God, insolent, haughty, boastful, inventors of evil, disobedient to parents, foolish, faithless, heartless, ruthless" (vv. 29-31). In other words, ingratitude takes you no place good.

This description should stop us in our tracks. Whereas some would say that gratitude is a simple courtesy, Scripture is clear that it's much more serious. An attitude of gratitude is one sure sign your heart is crucified to pride and selfishness and willing to acknowledge all that God is and does in your life. The thankful heart is a foundation for a godly life. To exercise faith by giving thanks is pleasing to God. When you thank Him for what you see, you are being faithful. When you thank Him for what you don't see, you are being faith filled (Heb. 11:6).

Cultivate the Discipline of Gratitude

Set aside time daily to express thanks to God. In ancient Israel a daily habit of thanksgiving was so important to the life of the nation that the Levites were officially appointed to stand in the temple every morning and evening to thank God (1 Chron. 23:30). In a more private context and a later generation, we find Daniel kneeling to thank God three times a day (Dan. 6:10).

As a way of cultivating an attitude of gratitude in your home, establish a family tradition. For example, before you eat a meal, take turns sharing something you're thankful for. Or as you tuck in the kids, talk about one thing that happened that day for which they are grateful. Sometimes this little discipline is difficult, especially if someone has had a difficulty.

Think back to the 10 lepers who were healed in Luke 17. Jesus said something curious to the one who came back to thank Him: "Rise and go your way; your faith has made you well" (v. 19). Didn't Jesus heal all 10? In what way did this one's faith make him well? Ten were healed physically; one was healed spiritually and eternally. Somehow the one leper's gratitude led to faith, and faith led to salvation. Scripture is full of accounts of people who recognize their dependence on God as the one who provides general blessings like life and breath, food and shelter. That simple gratitude is the tipping point of seeing our own sinfulness and our personal need for a Savior.

Faith grows in the soil of thankfulness. The first step is for a person who doesn't yet know Christ to acknowledge, "Yes there is a God. I have received much from His hand, and possibly I owe something to Him. I should be reconciled to this God who made me and gives me life and strength." At this point people will either acknowledge God for who He is, thank Him, and turn to Him in faith; or they will turn their backs on God and put themselves at the center of the universe.

It all hinges on gratitude. Romans 1:21 says that even though something deep within people tells them there is a God, a proud, ungrateful heart will not turn to Him. They won't acknowledge Him, and thereby they think they are not accountable to Him. "And their foolish hearts were darkened." All of the good things God wants to bring into their lives that follow repentance and faith, as Jesus referenced with the one thankful leper, are birthed in the soil of thankfulness. No wonder being thankful is commanded in Scripture.

> Read the following verses and write the reason believers need to be thankful
> Psalm 100:3
>
> Psalm 107:1
>
> John 3:16-17
>
> Colossians 2:6-7
>
> Hebrews 11:6

God commands us to be thankful because our gratitude is not based on whether we are enjoying life but on the realities of our lives in God; being filled with gratitude for who God is, for His Son, and for our salvation go deeper than any feelings drawn out of our experiences of pain or joy. Our thankful attitude is anchored in the assurances of our faith in Christ.

> List some of the certainties you have in Christ that fill you with gratitude. (Ex: Jesus died for my sins. My sins are forgiven. Nothing can separate me from God's love.) List related Scripture references when you know them.

When you feel yourself ready to despair or complain, return to these fixed realities in changing circumstances. This attitude of gratitude is the soil of faith.

Reason for Gratitude

My church funded a translation of the Jesus film into the language of an unreached people group in East Asia. They had never heard of Jesus or seen a movie. A few of us got to travel to see firsthand how these precious people would receive God's Word.

As we sat out in an open field, projecting the movie on a large white screen, we watched their amazement as they recognized the images and understood the story line. They were caught up in the curiosity of this new genre of storytelling, but they loved it. A few wandered behind the screen to see where the people had gone when they left the screen.

They pointed and laughed and commented as they followed the story. But when they saw this good man who healed sick people and tenderly talked to children get captured and led away, they stormed the screen, shaking their fists and yelling. Such rage at the injustice! They only quieted down when we assured them this wasn't the end of the story.

Next came the crucifixion. Again, they moaned with sorrow at what they saw for the first time. They wept and wailed and held each other in grief. We could hardly go on.

But we were completely unprepared for their response at the resurrection. With hardly a sound across the field where we sat, those of us who knew the triumphant end of this story waited. At the first sight of the risen Lord, the crowd erupted in joy. Celebration! They shouted and laughed and danced and hugged and pounded each other on the back! "He's alive," they screamed with joy. I'll never forget the joy.

It took a trip halfway around the world for me to realize that I had lost my awe and gratitude at what Jesus had done for me. I'm so grateful to have regained it, ironically, from the people I had prayed to reach with the gospel.

> *If somebody collected a dollar from you every time you complained and gave you one every time you showed gratitude, would you be rich or poor?*

For Discussion

1. What did this people group in East India understand about Jesus' death and resurrection that perhaps because of familiarity we often forget?

2. Some have said that Easter is a vast thank-you service. Humanly speaking, Jesus had no reason to come to this earth, but He came for one purpose: to die for a lost humanity. What did His sacrificial death accomplish on your behalf?

How has Jesus become your source of life?

3. "But thanks be to God, who in Christ always leads us in triumphal procession, and through us spreads the fragrance of the knowledge of him everywhere" (2 Cor. 2:14). This verse directs us to thank God for the victory we have because of Christ. Describe this victory.

Gratitude is a spiritual discipline. Just as a professional athlete must practice his sport, just as a chef must make a meal, just as an artist must paint a masterpiece or run scales on her piano, so must we practice the discipline of gratitude.

Thankfulness is a decision. It's a choice we make. "O that men would give thanks to the Lord" (Ps. 107:21, NKJV). What a critical, life-changing, joy-producing, happiness-inducing choice it really is. You can choose your attitude as much as you can choose your diet or your clothing.

What would it take for you to choose a thankful attitude?

Thankfulness is a decision based in reality.

Each of these verses indicates a choice to be thankful. What reason for being thankful is expressed in each verse?
Psalm 139:14

Isaiah 25:1

1 Corinthians 15:57

2 Corinthians 2:14

Colossians 3:15

Will you face the reality of your situation today with a thankful heart?

Thankfulness is a life-changing decision.

Reflect on your thinking in the past few days since we first began this study. Has there been a time when you purposed to be thankful rather than complain? What was your experience? How did you sense God at work?

Will you allow a thankful attitude to change your actions?

Are you reading your "I am thankful for ..." list that you created earlier this week? Expand your list today, and keep reviewing it.

Begin the discipline of a prayer time each day that is only thanksgiving to God. Don't ask for a thing. Save your petitions for another time of prayer at some other time in the day. Read Scripture back to God, sing a worship song, keep a list of reasons He is worthy of your praise and thanksgiving. Fill the entire time just thanking Him. Tomorrow extend your thanksgiving time even longer.

Lord, forgive my proud heart when I've not remembered or refused to give You thanks. I am completely dependent on You for life and breath, for salvation and forgiveness, and for the hope of eternal life. Penetrate my heart with these truths. Empty my heart of pride, and fill it with thankfulness to You every day of my life from this day forward. Amen.

WEEK 2. DAY 5. WRAPPING UP THE BLESSINGS OF A THANKFUL ATTITUDE

Several years ago I came across the story of a pastor named Ed Dobson. His church in the Midwest was making a real impact. In the middle of that success, Pastor Dobson got sick, and some pretty ominous clouds began to gather over his life. When the final details were known, he was diagnosed with Lou Gehrig's disease, a degenerative disease of the nervous system that causes your muscles to atrophy, eventually taking your capacity to speak and ultimately to breathe. Doctors can do nothing—no medication, no therapy, no treatment, no nothing. They tell you to go home or go back to work and wait. You're going to die in three to five years.

I read an interview with Pastor Dobson as he shared the news that he had a few weeks or months left to live on this earth. One question the interviewer asked him was, "How has this knowledge that you're going to die changed your prayer life?" He said, "Well, it's not what you think. It's not that every day I ask God to heal me, though I have prayed that prayer. The major change in my prayer life is that most of my prayers now are prayers of gratitude as opposed to long lists of requests. I'm just happy to be alive! I'm happy to be able to do everything and anything that I'm able to do; I'm thankful for it."

Pastor Dobson's attitude brings before us again the reality that a follower of Jesus Christ is the most thankful person on the face of the earth, thankful for every person and for every circumstance. But it takes us faith to say the words, "God is using this. I don't know why God's allowed this, but He's using it. He is eternal and a sovereign God; He knows what He's doing, and I trust Him."

Here's the final principle we need to grasp in our study of gratitude: We must see every person or circumstance as God's coming to us through that person or circumstance to make us more like His Son, Jesus Christ. No doubt about it, the hardest word in that statement is *every*. God has all of us in some kind of training program. Should I be grateful for the harsh thing? the hurtful person? that great disappointment? Yes. Learn to see every person or circumstance as God coming to me through that situation, growing me up, transforming me to look more like His Son. None of those things touch my life except that God allows it and is using it. He is in control of everything.

This is a building block of Christian character. God is at work in the ugly to produce the beautiful. God is at work in the painful to bring about something good. God is at work in the wrong to do the right. God is at work in the bad to produce the good. This is the confidence of the follower of Jesus Christ. Do you have a sense that God is for you?

Cultivating a Thankful Attitude in the Past, Present, and Future

We need to learn to "give thanks in all circumstances; for this is the will of God in Christ Jesus for you" (1 Thess. 5:18). To thank God for all things is to stand on a height and see the beginning and the end. Not only is this a spiritual discipline that we must practice all the time, but it is also an act of faith. First we must look back …

Be Grateful for What God Has Done

A bad memory is an insult to God. To forget what to be thankful for is to forget God's goodness. It's to shrink His character and minimize His power. Think back to a season of uncertainty in your life and consider the goodness of God in how life has developed since then. What fears have been unmasked as frauds? What wasted time was spent anxious or worried about something that never happened? Live from now on knowing that life is going to turn out OK no matter what. How can you be so confident? Because you know God is in charge. We don't thank Him enough because we forget all that He's done.

Jesus said to cultivate your memory. "And when he had given thanks, he broke it, and said, 'This is my body which is for you. Do this in remembrance of me.' In the same way also he took the cup, after supper, saying, 'This cup is the new covenant in my blood. Do this, as often as you drink it, in remembrance of me' " (1 Cor. 11:24-25).

Jesus said we should remember and be grateful for all He did to pay for our sin. The next time you participate in the Lord's Supper, remember and thank God for all He has done for you.

Be Grateful for What God Is Doing

Do you get caught up in the myopia of the moment? Do you only see the depressing present and not the hopeful future? Give thanks! "Give thanks in all circumstances" (1 Thess. 5:18).

Telling someone broken by sorrow to rejoice or be joyful is like telling someone handicapped by some crushing blow to walk by walking. But there is great wisdom (really, pure genius!) in this command. We don't see in order to give thanks; we give thanks in order to see. No matter how difficult any present situation, nothing can compare with what God is planning.

> What offering of hope does Romans 1:18 extend?
>
> What hope does 2 Corinthians 4:16-18 offer?
>
> How does the phrase, "We don't see in order to give thanks; we give thanks in order to see," apply to the habit of a thankful attitude?

Be Grateful for What God Will Do

Last week in our study we read about the children of Israel on the run from the Egyptian army with their backs up against the Red Sea. They were in a panic. Moses said, "Do not be afraid. Stand firm and you will see the deliverance the Lord will bring you today. The Egyptians you see today you will never see again. The Lord will fight for you; you need only to be still" (Ex. 14:13-14, NIV). And God came through just as Moses said. The waters of the sea miraculously parted, the army drowned, and the people danced for joy on the other side.

How great would it have been if they had believed God and danced on the Egyptian side of the Red Sea? The Egyptian bullies would have been doubly defeated, God doubly glorified, and their joy intensified. The discipline of giving thanks in all circumstances is an act of hope. When we give thanks no matter what, we act on the premise that the future will turn out OK. The next moment might not be great, even the next year; but God has assured us that everything will be glorious in the end.

What assurance does Romans 5:2-5 give that God knows what He is doing and we can trust Him, and even thank Him for difficult times?

Why should you be certain of this? Because God is good all the time. He rewards faithfulness and faith. Everything God promises about the future is true. You act in a way you believe that is true when you give thanks.

For the follower of Jesus Christ, a thankful attitude begins and ends with seeing the goodness of the Lord. Begin the habit of rehearsing God's grace in your life by visiting Psalm 103 often. Read it now. List all the reasons you have to be thankful for His character. Make it personal.

Thank You, Lord, for ...

When a prayer is answered or something wonderful happens, before you talk to anyone else, go to God immediately and thank Him.

As you reflect over this week's focus on gratitude, you may notice exercises listing things for which you are or need to be thankful. Rehearsing the goodness of God is a discipline, like an attitude, developed over a long time.

Remember the list at the beginning of the week of people, spiritual blessings, and other areas for which you are thankful? Did you read the list before every meal and bedtime? If you did, what was your experience? Any change in attitude? What was your attitude during the process?

What God Is Showing You

Think back over our areas of focus this week and reflect on what God is teaching you about how to replace a complaining attitude with a thankful attitude ...

• Gratitude is the attitude that sets the altitude for living.
• You can thank God even when you don't feel thankful.
• The discipline of gratitude is the explicit effort to acknowledge that all you are and have is a gift of love from God and a gift to be celebrated.
• To be grateful is to recognize God's hand on everything that touches your life.
• God's will for your life is to be thankful.
• A thankful attitude is a big deal to Jesus.
• Gratitude consists of being more aware of what you have than what you don't.
• Faith grows in the soil of thankfulness.
• Thankfulness is a decision.
• Thankfulness is a decision based on reality.
• Thankfulness is a life-changing decision.
• Be grateful for what God has done.
• Be grateful for what God is doing.
• Be grateful for what God will do.

REPLACE A COVETOUS ATTITUDE ...

Group Activity

Give each person a piece of paper and a pen or pencil. Tell them to list 10 things for which they are thankful. Instruct them to draw a line following each of the 10 items.

When everyone has their list, tell them to find someone who has one of the same items and to sign their name on the line by that item.

Discuss briefly items the group found named most frequently and the items that were unique to one person's list.

Discussion Questions
About Thankfulness

1. Why is gratitude such a big deal?
2. How did Jesus' parable about the lepers illustrate sincere gratitude?
3. Are you thankful for what God has given you?
4. What is the root and fruit of gratitude?
5. How can you grow in expressing gratitude?

Video

We go back to the desert to look at the attitude of coveteousness. Watch and listen for what covetousness does in a believer's life.

Video Notes

Those who choose _____ as their lifestyle will spend their lifetime in the wilderness.

Covetousness is wanting _____ things.

Covetousness is wanting _____ things for the wrong reason.

Covetousness is wanting right things but at the wrong _____.

Covetousness is wanting right things but in the wrong _____.

Act 1: Yielding to Covetousness and Why God _____ It

1. Covetousness becomes _____ when you yield.

2. When we dwell on _____, yielding is only a matter of time.

3. At the root of covetousness is a rejection of God's _____.

Act 2: A _____ from God You Don't Want

Beware of begging God for _____.

If you're covetous person, _____ is never enough.

If you're a covetous person, you'll spend your life in the _____.

1. Why does God hate covetousness?
2. James MacDonald says that covetousness becomes active sin only when we yield. Do you agree with this? Why or why not?
3. What are the consequences of having a covetous attitude?

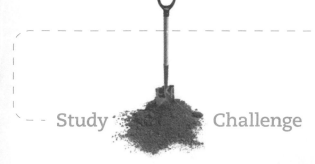

Discussion Questions
About a Covetous Attitude

Study   Challenge

Do you have a covetous attitude? This week's study will delve into Scripture and help you apply biblical truths to your life to see if you are covetous and, if so, what you can do about it.

Memory Verse

"Store up for yourselves treasures in heaven, where neither moth nor rust destroys, and where thieves do not break in or steal; for where your treasure is, there will your heart be also."
Matthew 6:20-21, NASB

Most of us don't see ourselves as greedy. As fun as it is to play *Who Wants to Be a Millionaire?* or *Deal or No Deal,* we're not obsessed with the thought of being rich. The more subtle game we play in our heads is the preoccupation with "if only":

If only I made a little more money …
If only we could get a bigger/better car … house …
If only I could have more …

Deep down we've convinced ourselves that life would be better if we had just a little more. So we live forever discontented—forever craving, grasping, wishing, wanting, and striving for that next thing. This thirst for more is exactly what the Bible describes as greed or covetousness. In our first lesson in this study, we looked at complaining. It was this craving for their own desires that sent the children of Israel wandering into the desert for the rest of their lives. They couldn't be happy with all the miracles God provided; they could only be satisfied with what they wanted and more of it until it killed them.

Covetousness is like a thirsty man drinking salt water, which only makes him thirstier, which causes him to drink more … until ultimately it kills him. Our nation and our neighborhoods are drowning in a sea of covetousness. You and I are part of it more than we realize. We may even think this greed topic isn't necessarily our problem. We may have even deceived ourselves into thinking we live in victory over our own materialistic desires. But that's only compared to the people around us. Truth is, we are all at such a desperate place that it's hard even to be objective about it.

Clearly Jesus said, "A man's life does not consist in the abundance of his possessions" (Luke 12:15, NIV). Life is not about stuff. The sooner we get that in our heads, the more satisfied our hearts will be. Unfortunately, greed is a big fat liar that says, "Just a little more and your life will be complete." Don't believe it.

> More of anything other than God will never fill that longing for fulfillment He has placed within you and me that is satisfied in Him alone

Is this coveting? What do <u>you</u> think?
☐ Yes ☐ No   I see that my neighbor has a new car. From his choice of make/model to the color of interior, I love it! As I walk back to my house, I think, *I wish I could afford a new car. But I really can't right now. Oh, well, when I can, that's the car I want!*

☐ Yes ☐ No   I want to be married more than anything else in the world. I sit in church and watch married couples worship together and hold hands when they pray; it makes me want a spouse even more. I can't take it anymore. I'm quitting church.

☐ Yes ☐ No   Why can't I ever get ahead? I work, save, and hunt for bargains and never seem to have what I want. Why do I miss out when other people get their houses, trips, jewelry, and private schools? It's just not right.

Coveting is a powerful and underestimated sin. It can cripple you spiritually and ultimately destroy you. It must not be underestimated or left unchecked.

What Is Covetousness?

Covetousness is:

- Wanting *wrong* things.
- Wanting *right* things for the *wrong* reasons.
- Wanting *right* things at the *wrong* time.
- Wanting *right* things in the *wrong* amount.

Let's get specific.

- Covetousness is wanting wrong things like power, control, wealth, success at any cost, esteem at any cost, or glory and praise.
- It is wanting right things for the wrong reasons like leadership (for control) or to be spiritual (for the reputation).
- It is wanting right things at the wrong time like a lovely home (but with drowning debt) or marital intimacy (but before marriage).
- It is wanting right things in the wrong amount like money (more of it) or influence (in dangerous amounts).

1. Think about your first job—what were your wages, your needs, and your priorities? Consider how the years have changed those things for the better or worse. How has your attitude toward your salary, your needs, and your priorities changed?

2. Think of how much time and energy you spend sorting, transporting, buying, and maintaining your stuff. Remember the last time you moved your household? Or if that's been a while, what does your garage, attic, closets, and storage unit look like? Is your stuff getting in the way of what you really want to do with your life? How do you know?

When Does Wanting Something Become Sin?

It is *impossible* not to desire things, experiences, and situations. The question is, when does wanting go too far? When does it become sin? When you yield to it. When you give it the right of way.

The passage we've been studying in Numbers 11:4 (NKJV) says, "The mixed multitude who were among them yielded to intense craving." They gave in to those desires. Romans 8:5 (NKJV) says,

"Those who live according to the flesh set their minds on the things of the flesh. But those who live according to the Spirit, the things of the Spirit."

Is it sin to want certain things? No, but it becomes sin when you give in to it, when you yield to that desire and let it have the right of way.

Warning Signs of Covetousness

Read Deuteronomy 8:17-18. When I forget who gave me _____ and to whom it ultimately belongs.

Read Psalm 106:21-22. When I _____ how God provided for me in the past and only look at what I don't have today.

Read Matthew 6:25. When instead of managing my stuff, I become _____ over it.

Read 2 Corinthians 9:7. When I no longer _____ cheerfully.

Read 1 Peter 2:1. When I look around at what others have and I become _____ for it.

Greed is not merely wanting material things; it's an obsession. Covetous people are preoccupied with the things of this world, care too much about things they can't buy, dream about their next acquisition, and are frustrated if they can't get what they want when they want it.

When we yield, we give in to things that shouldn't be a part of our lives or shouldn't be a part of our lives at that time or in that amount.

Wise Warnings

The most common form of coveting is motivated by the love of money. "The love of money is a root of all kinds of evils. It is through this craving that some have wandered away from the faith and pierced themselves with many pangs" (1 Tim. 6:10).

Answer the questions that follow:

1. Does this verse say that having money is evil? Clarify.

2. What is the caution raised here? How does this "evil root" differ from a healthy desire to support yourself and your family and be successful in your work and investments?

Things were never designed to take God's place. When we covet something and make it essential, then beg God to give it to us, we are asking God to replace Himself with something we consider more important. When we do this, God will often allow us to experience firsthand the consequences of substituting anything for Him.

3. Describe what could be included in "all kinds of evil."

4. This verse describes the love of money as "craving." Describe how this parallels the children of Israel's "craving" for food in the Numbers 11.

5. Look at the verses before and after 1 Timothy 6:10. What warning do verses 6-9 pose about pursuing wealth as the primary ambition of your life?

What does verse 11 say a godly person should go after instead of riches?

Search My Heart, O Lord

Father, You tell me in Your Word that every good and perfect gift is from You. I thank You for all that You've given to me. I think now of _____. You've blessed me beyond what I need. I see now that covetousness has been a hidden pattern in my life. I confess to You that _____

_____

_____.

Lord, please give me eyes to see my true condition and the spiritual poverty that comes with the pursuit of material wealth. God, don't let me live for that. Don't let me spend my time for that. Bring freedom into my life that comes from submission to Your truth. Give me a heart to believe that even right now this is an appointment with You. Might I hear Your voice clearly about _____

_____.

Some sins are more easily detected than others and more often condemned by those professing godliness. But covetousness is too often only winked at, and some covetous persons are regarded as respectable people. *Is it really a sin?* That's what many people ask, including Christians. How could an appetite for more be all that bad?

While the world applauds greed as legitimate ambition, as business shrewdness, or as a competitive bent, all kinds of excuses are made for Christians to write off this insatiable push for more as simply a character flaw or loss of priority. But hear me now: the Bible puts covetousness in the big list.

"You shall not covet your neighbor's house; you shall not covet your neighbor's wife, or his male servant, or his female servant, or his ox, or his donkey, or anything that is your neighbor's" (Ex. 20:17).

While the other Commandments deal with things we do outwardly, this one has to do with what we do inwardly; and while the other Commandments deal with forbidden actions, this one deals with forbidden attitudes. When you confess your sin to the Lord, do you ever include your dissatisfaction with what God has given you and your greed for more? Do you want to right now?

Look up the following verses and get a broad view of God's opinion of covetousness.

1. In Joshua 7:20-26 and Job 31:24-25,28, God feels this way:

2. In Mark 7:21-23, God puts covetousness in a category with what other sins?

3. What does 1 Timothy 6:9 say covetousness causes in a person's heart?

4. What does James 4:1-3 say covetousness causes in the church?

5. How does God describe His heart toward Israel's coveting in Isaiah 57:17?

Will we be grateful and satisfied with God and His provision for us? Or will we covet more and better and different?

6. What do Colossians 3:5 and Ephesians 5:5 call covetousness? Why?

7. According to Psalm 52:7, why would God be so angry about this sin in particular?

Put yourself to the test. Spend some time before the Lord, asking Him to show you places in your life that have been under the control of a covetous attitude. Then, still prayerful and repentant, walk about your house and surrender specifics to Him. What about your home has been established out of a desire for "more"? Look at the diplomas on your walls or your briefcase and computer. What about your education or your career has been a substitute for more of God in your life? Stop at every place where the Spirit prompts and surrender it to the Lord. "Lord, I once thought this would satisfy, but now I see that only You can. I surrender this _____ to You. Take away this desire and fill me instead with Your Spirit."

Think of some of the people in the Bible who threw it all away because of greed and covetousness.

Genesis 3:1-7: _____ threw it all away in order to gain _____.

Joshua 7:21: _____ threw it all away in order to gain _____.

1 Kings 21: _____ threw it all away in order to gain _____.

2 Kings 5: _____ threw it all away in order to gain _____.

Matthew 26:15; 27:3-5: _____ threw it all away in order to gain _____.

Acts 5:1-11: _____ threw it all away in order to gain _____.

Consequences

Some lost their lives, some lost fellowship with God, and some lost their reputation. In their attempt to gain what God had not given them, everyone lost something big.

In your experience or observation, what do people lose today in their pursuit of more?

It's payday again.

You sit at the kitchen table with a stack of bills, a checkbook, and a whole lot of questions. When will we ever get ahead? Which bill can we let slip this month? We've got a little leftover. What should we do with it?

If your bank statement could talk, it would tell a big piece of your life story—your priorities, your strengths, and your weaknesses. It could even describe the location and condition of your heart.

Your attitude toward money and the practical, financial management of all the resources God has provided you and your family play a huge part of godly, purposeful living. Matched with wisdom, a spirit of generosity, and the desire to apply what the Scripture says about money, your financial management provides a realistic indicator of your spiritual maturity. *Money does talk.*

What is yours saying?

Covetousness, rampant in the Western world and in the evangelical church, blocks the flow of God's fullness in our lives.

WEEK 3. DAY 3. MORE ISN'T BETTER

In the New Testament Jesus said more about money than He said about heaven and hell put together. He talked about finances all the time. Of His 38 parables 16 are about finances—how to use money and how to keep it from using and abusing you. The New Testament has five hundred verses on prayer, fewer than five hundred verses on faith, but more than two thousand dealing with "me and my stuff."

Coveting includes giving anything other than God our best affection and our highest attention.

That's not to say that money is the most important subject in Scripture; it isn't. But it is a critical issue and the thing that often enslaves our hearts when God wants to own all that we are.

While we're focused on discerning what could be a covetous attitude in our hearts, do you wonder if this could be an issue in your life after all? Jesus taught five specific principles in Luke 12 that will help direct your heart toward Him.

1. More is not better. Jesus said that man's "life does not consist in the abundance of the things he possesses" (v. 15, NKJV). You say, "I know life isn't about stuff!" But saying it and living it are very different. It is all tied back to whether you really believe what the Bible says or think that somehow more stuff is going to enhance your life.

People who have more are not necessarily happier. If you have more square footage, you're not happier because of it. If you have a nicer car or better clothes or more exotic vacations, you are not happier because of them. I've fellowshipped with people around the world who live in shelters you wouldn't store your gardening supplies in; and they have bigger smiles, more joyful worship, and a greater sense of God's fullness than some of us have ever known! More is not better. In fact, the bulk in our bank accounts and the poverty of our souls indicates that many times more is worse.

☐ Yes ☐ No   Do you agree?
☐ Yes ☐ No   Do you think "more" is sometimes worse?
☐ Yes ☐ No   Has this been your experience?

2. Hoarding is for fools. Covetousness can sometimes be seen when you hoard your income instead of generously sharing it. Jesus calls the person who does this a fool. "So is he who lays up treasure for himself and is not rich toward God" (v. 21, NKJV). Hear Jesus' heart in this matter. He is asking, "Why are you doing that?" Life is suddenly over, and you invested in what doesn't last. It's foolish.

How do you think verses 21 and 34 relate to each other?

You say, "What if I really began to give generously, what would I go without? What about my retirement? What would my kids go without? It gets complicated."

Jesus anticipated our concern about generous giving; in verses 22 and 28 He said, "Therefore I say to you, do not worry about your life, what you will eat; nor about the body, what you will put on. … If then God so clothes the grass, which today is in the field and tomorrow is thrown into the oven, how much more will He clothe you, O you of little faith" (NKJV).

Jesus said, "You don't trust Me very much, do you? Do you think that God is going to leave you behind because you put Him first?" This whole matter of giving is about faith. When the offering plate goes by every week at church, you make a choice to give and trust God, or you hoard and do not trust God. Do you give 10 percent off the top as He has asked you to do? Or do you keep most of it just in case God doesn't supply your needs? It's a matter of faith.

Really, it's asking the question, "God, does everything that I have belong to You?"

3. You can't outgive God. Jesus didn't tell us to give generously because He wants us to sweat. Rather, He wants us to experience our inability to outgive God. He said, "And your Father knows that you need these things. But seek first the kingdom of God, and all these things shall be added to you" (v. 31, NKJV). Have you ever given generously, out of sacrifice even, and seen God multiply it back in blessings? I have. Sometimes it returns financially, and sometimes it returns in other spiritual blessings, but it always returns!

Have you seen this to be true in your life? When?

God Almighty will not be in a debt position to you. Do you know what it is to trust Him, to obey Him, and to see Him meet all of your needs? It's phenomenal!

Take your wallet out of your pocket or purse and get it in your hands. (Really!) This is a symbol of all that God has given to you. Hold that symbol as you read Luke 12:31: "Seek first the kingdom of God and all these things shall be added to you" (NKJV). On the heels of that familiar verse, Jesus said these tender words, "Do not fear, little flock" (v. 32). That's the only time in the whole New Testament that He calls us "little flock." Jesus is so tender. He knows we get really protective when we get our money in our hands. "Oh no! What if I go without?" and He says, "Do not fear, little flock. For it is your Father's good pleasure to give you the kingdom."

Then He said, "Sell what you have and give alms" (v. 33). This doesn't mean liquidate everything; otherwise we would all be on government assistance. What Jesus meant is, "Don't let your buying habits leave you in a position where you can't give." Then He compared earthly investments to heavenly investment. "Provide for yourselves money bags which do not grow old, a treasure in the heavens that does not fail where no thief approaches nor moth destroys."

Have you ever sacrificed or worked overtime in order to buy something only to be disappointed in it somehow? ☐ Yes ☐ No What was it?

Have you ever given your money to God and been disappointed?

4. What you cherish reveals your heart. When you can't take your eyes off the stock market because your security is in your investments, you are in bondage to money. When your dreams for the future are things to own or places to visit and not people to impact, you are in bondage to money.

In light of all this, I'm sure you have questions. "Should I buy a better car?" "We're tithing, and we have some cash. We want to buy a vacation home. Should we do that?" I don't have any answers except for this next verse. I'll let you wrestle with it. Jesus said, "For where your treasure is, there your heart will be also" (v. 34, NKJV). Jesus said, "Be careful" because the more you accumulate, the greater the tendency for your heart to get drawn away.

When deep in your heart you believe that more money would make you happier and getting more money is your highest priority, you are in bondage to finances.

Is this a timely verse to hear right now? Why/why not?

5. The time to give is now. "Stay dressed for action," Jesus said, "and keep your lamps burning, and be like men who are waiting for their master to come home from the wedding feast, so that they may open the door to him at once when he comes" (Luke 12:35-36). Get up, get the lights on, and get ready. Jesus could come back at any moment. "If he comes in the second watch, or in the third, and finds them awake, blessed are those servants!" (v. 38). If you have been faithful to God in money matters, you will be blessed for your faithfulness.

I've been in the ministry a long time, and I've never worried about the financial needs of God's kingdom. God is not in heaven saying, "How are we going to pay these bills? We really need the people of God to come through for us!" That's backwards. I'm passionate about seeing people get free who think that the next thing they buy or the next vacation they take is going to make them happy. Nothing but living for and obeying Christ is going to turn that key. May God give you the courage to put Him first and to experience the marvelous provision reserved for those who obey His Word.

Some of us are like that little English boy who lived in the darkness of the tunnels under the streets of London. He never saw the light of day until someone found him, took him by the hand up a stairway and out into the beautiful world of trees and lakes and sky. Some of you have been living in the darkness of covetousness. I long for you to experience the joy of making what God has given you available to Him and leaving behind the wilderness of covetousness.

Does this describe your attitude right now? How would you like to change or press on in what you're already doing?

Before going any further, let's look at the whole picture. What are you really thinking about covetousness? Be honest.

Is ingratitude really as serious as all that?

☐ Agree ☐ Disagree
☐ Agree ☐ Disagree

In time you may come to hate the very thing you had to have. We are not only in bondage to covetousness, but we are in serious denial about it.

Covetousness includes these five areas:

1. Coveting material things, money, and things money can buy
Read 1 Timothy 6:10.
Should a Christian be wealthy?

What distinction does this verse make that determines whether money is a problem?

2. Coveting status or position
Read Luke 22:24.
What kind of covetousness does this verse say the disciples struggled with?

3. Coveting your own agenda
Read 1 Thessalonians 2:5-6.
In what way was Paul not guilty of covetousness?

4. Coveting after people—wanting what I can't have, desiring what would go against God's law
Read Matthew 5:28 and Ephesians 5:3.
How do these verses illustrate covetousness?

5. Coveting power
Read Acts 8:18-19.
What did Simon the magician really want to buy?

Why was that important to him?

Which of these five types of coveting do you struggle with?

Warnings Against Covetousness

Covetousness is like a thirsty man drinking salt water. You think it will quench your need, but it causes dehydration and death. It can't satisfy.

Read and answer the following questions to discover how Scripture explains covetousness the same way.

1. Covetousness never brings satisfaction.
Read Ecclesiastes 5:11 and Luke 12:15.
Do you know people—or perhaps this describes you—who have everything this world offers yet are not satisfied? How would you describe their lives?

☐ Agree ☐ Disagree   Money doesn't satisfy those who love it.

Luke 12:15 says a satisfied life isn't about stuff. Where do you say a satisfied life comes from?

2. Covetousness hinders your spiritual life.
Read Mark 4:1–20.
In this parable of the soils, Jesus described seed that got choked out. How do verses 18-19 explain the effect of covetousness?

What should be our first response to God's Word when we hear it taught?

3. Covetousness leads to other sins.
According to 1 Timothy 6:10 and James 4:2, how is covetousness a breeding ground for a thousand other sins?

4. Covetousness lets you down when you need help most.
Read 1 Timothy 6:7.
What does this say about the value of covetousness at your moment of need?

Think about it. If your life should suddenly end today, will you stand before God with great joy in Him or with a spiritual cavity where your stuff used to be?

5. Covetousness destroys the soul.
Read 1 Timothy 6:9.
How do you think covetousness sets us up for destruction? In our marriages, in our jobs, in our faith (v. 10)?

COVETOUSNESS IS
Wanting **wrong** things.

Wanting right things
for the **wrong** reasons.

Wanting right things
at the **wrong** time.

Wanting right things
in the **wrong** amount.

Case Study in Covetousness

I never thought I had a problem with covetousness, but maybe I do. I was at the mall this week; and before I knew it, I was in one of my favorite stores. I was standing in front of the jewelry counter, looking at a nice watch. I didn't need a watch, but it was so delicate and had pretty diamonds around the face. I stood there for a long time, knowing I couldn't afford it but wanting it all the same. I rationalized how I could pay for it and why I deserved it. I wrestled with myself. "You don't need this watch. Next week you won't event remember it." Yeah, but I wanted it now. So I quickly bought it and left the store.

A few minutes later as I walked toward my car in the mall parking lot, I felt just awful. I had caved in to covetousness. The Spirit was telling me to correct my problem right away while I was still feeling badly. So I turned around, walked back into the mall, and back to the store. I had hoped not to get the same sales clerk, but there she stood. "I'd like to return the watch," I said. "Is something wrong?" "No, in fact it's all good," I said and walked out with mixed feelings.

I felt sad that my pattern had continued but glad that I had eventually done the right thing. I prayed, "Lord, I typically use things like this watch to gratify myself, but now I offer my time and my money to You. Give me someone to minister to right now. Lord, show me somebody that I can encourage. Give me a way to use my life and myself for You. I offer myself to You in this moment." And of course, our faithful God did just that. He gave me an opportunity to serve Him later the same day that I probably would have missed had I been nursing my feelings of guilt. I'm determined to obey Him, even if I have to retrace my steps to make it right.

Can you identify with the struggle that this sister in Christ felt at the mall?

When was the last time you wrestled with a decision to buy something that would feed your feelings of covetousness?

What did you do?

What godly advice can you offer fellow Christians in the area of temptation against covetousness?

WEEK 3. DAY 5. WRAPPING UP: THE SOLUTION TO COVETOUSNESS

We've spent four days looking into the bottomless, empty well of covetousness. Once you look for satisfaction anywhere but where God promises that you will find it, it's an ever-searching, never-finding pursuit.

It's drinking all the water in the world and your thirst is still unquenched.
It's eating every delicacy you can find and it tasting like sand.

Solomon discovered the foolishness of seeking satisfaction apart from God. Tongue-in-cheek he wrote in his journal, "Bread is made for laughter, and wine gladdens life, and money answers everything" (Eccl. 10:19). If he had lived in this generation, he would have added a sarcastic, "Not!"

Nobody ever pursued possessing like Solomon; yet at the end of his life, he turned to God, repented of his doubting ways and became satisfied in God and His good gifts. He said of his experience: "Behold, what I have seen to be good and fitting is to eat and drink and find enjoyment in all the toil with which one toils under the sun the few days of his life that God has given him, for this is his lot. Everyone also to whom God has given wealth and possessions and power to enjoy them, and to accept his lot and rejoice in his toil—this is the gift of God. For he will not much remember the days of his life because God keeps him occupied with joy in his heart" (Eccl. 5:18-20).

1. In your own words, describe how Solomon answered his longing for more, and better, and other apart from God?

2. What did he see as the solution?

3. What did Solomon say to the wealthy?

4. How did Solomon think God answers the problem of covetousness?

5. How do these verses encourage or challenge you?

Solomon learned that the opposite of covetousness is contentment in God. When contentment in God decreases, covetousness for gain increases. Paul took another approach, saying that covetousness is idolatry: "Put to death therefore what is earthly in you: sexual immorality, impurity, passion, evil desire, and covetousness, which is idolatry" (Col. 3:5).

If *idolatry* means "putting anything else in God's place," why would Paul describe covetousness as an idol?

Why do you think God put it in His "top 10" Commandment list? (Ex. 20:17)?

Why is He making such a big deal out of it?

Covetousness is wanting something so much that you lose your satisfaction in God. It's looking elsewhere for what only God can give.

A Challenge for Faith

Earlier in our study we looked closely at 1 Timothy 6:10: "For the love of money is a root of all kinds of evils. It is through this craving that some have wandered away from the faith and pierced themselves with many pangs."

In the next verse, we read the warning to run from the love of money and the desire to be rich—namely, covetousness. Instead of giving in to covetousness, "As for you, O man of God, flee these things. Pursue righteousness, godliness, faith, love, steadfastness, gentleness" (v. 11).

Instead of giving in to your covetous desires, Paul is urging us to run after godly things. Then Paul singles out one character trait: faith. "Fight the good fight of faith" (v. 12). In other words, the fight against covetousness is nothing other than the fight of faith. When you think about it, covetousness implies that God is not enough. You have to go seek your satisfaction elsewhere. Yet what does Jesus say in John 6:35?

The fight of faith is the fight to keep your heart contented in Christ—to believe and then keep on believing that He will meet every need and satisfy every longing. When you crave something other than Him, put on the brakes. Before going forward, ask yourself: What do I not believe about what God has promised me? Where did I get off track? And finally, tell Him, "I want to get back to You, God. Please help me." Why not do that right now?

When covetousness begins to raise its ugly head, preach the Word of God to yourself. Remember what God has said. Hear His warnings about how serious it is to covet. Hear His promises for satisfaction that conquers every craving for more or better or anything other than what He has given us.

WITH
CONTENTMENT

In small groups of five or six, let someone toss out a category and the entire group will respond with things for which they are thankful. For example, someone might say "people." Group members might respond with, "Thank You, Lord, for my pastor." "Thank You, Lord, for my spouse." "Thank You, Lord, for my doctor."

1. Isn't everyone greedy to a certain extent?

2. Are you taking the sin of covetousness seriously?

3. How can you tell if you have a coveting problem?

4. How does covetousness affect your entire life?

5. What is your way of escape from the temptation of covetousness?

Discussion Questions
About a Covetous Attitude

Video

Watch and listen for how you can change your attitude from covetousness to contentment.

Video Notes

The opposite of covetousness is **contentment**.

Contentment— **satisfaction** in God's sufficient provision, to rest in what one has and seek nothing more.

Godliness + Contentment = Great Gain

Faulty Formulas
1. Godliness + **Prosperity** = Great Gain
2. Godliness + **Poverty** = Great Gain
3. Godliness + **Power** = Great Gain
4. Godliness + **Family Harmony** = Great Gain
5. Godliness + Ministry **Success** = Great Gain

Motivations
1. Look to _eternity_.
2. Let _enough_ be enough.
3. Learn by _example_.

Keys to Contentment
1 _Seek_ it.
2. _Say_ it.
3. _Settle_ it.

Money allows you to go places and do things and experience pressures to sin that someone in poverty will never know.

1. Do you agree or disagree that covetousness and contentment are opposites. Why? _Yes_

2. How does contentment or seeking nothing more resonate with contemporary culture?

3. Which of the Faulty Formulas have you encountered most often? What makes that formula faulty?

4. Which of the motivations works best for you?

5. What is the conflict between money and contentment?

Discussion Questions
About a Contentment

Study Challenge

Are you content with your place and possessions? This week's study will take a look at relevant Scripture passages and help you apply biblical truths to your life to see if you can grow in an attitude of contentment.

WEEK 4. DAY 1. CONTENTMENT

Memory Verse

"Now there is great gain in godliness with contentment, for we brought nothing into the world, and we cannot take anything out of the world. But if we have food and clothing, with these we will be content. But those who desire to be rich fall into temptation, into a snare, into many senseless and harmful desires that plunge people into ruin and destruction. For the love of money is a root of all kinds of evils. It is through this craving that some have wandered away from the faith and pierced themselves with many pangs."
1 Timothy 6:6-10

Contentment. It's a nice word, isn't it? Pause right now and take a deep breath. Inhale the crisp, clean air of a contented lifestyle.

After our study last week about our greedy, short-sighted, selfish, covetous attitudes and always wanting more and better and different, we will enjoy this week on the flip side of that attitude and discover how to make the moment-by-moment choice for contentment. What is contentment and how do we get there? The wilderness attitude of covetousness says, "It's not enough, God." The promised land attitude of contentment says, "You're enough, God."

Let's start with a definition: Contentment—Satisfaction in God's Sufficient Provision

Satisfied. You don't need anything else. You're satisfied with what God has entrusted to you. You have enough. Talk about going against the grain of the culture! Contentment means to rest in what one already has and seek nothing more, to say without fear of the future or envy of others, "I have enough." Contentment is like a cup of cold water to a man in a desert. Get it? Desert means thirst. Coveting means wilderness. Contentment is the promised land!

When we left the children of Israel wandering in the wilderness, they were caught up in the "we want more" attitude. What lessons do you suppose God wanted to teach them by providing only enough manna for their daily needs and no more?

Pause right now and ponder what lessons God might want to teach you as we explore this personal subject. Open your hands on the table or on your lap and surrender in prayer to Him as we begin.

Do you believe it is possible to be satisfied and content when circumstances are less than ideal?
☐ **Yes** ☐ **No** Why? Why not?

On the scale below, indicate how consistently you have been content in your circumstances during the past five years.

1	2	3	4	5	6	7	8	9	10
Very Inconsistently								Very Consistently	

Has your capacity to be content increased or decreased over the years? Why?

What situations or attitudes in your life produce discontent? How do these things keep you from being content?

What are the potential consequences of discontentment?

Name three things you're thankful for right now:
1.

2.

3.

> Contentment is ...
> • A satisfaction with what God has provided.
> • To rest in what you have and to seek nothing more.
> • A settled sense of adequacy.

Trapped in Wilderness Thinking

What about you? Do you sometimes feel trapped in wilderness thinking? Read the scenarios below. Do any of them remind you of you? In each scenario someone is saying, "God, what You've provided isn't enough."

"I want to serve God full-time, but I would have to sell our big house just when we've got it looking great." Trapped!

"I want to spend more time with my family and pursue eternal priorities, but in my company everyone at my level works 60 hours a week. If I don't keep up, I'll lose my status." Trapped!

"I don't want to spend so much money on clothing and cars, but we have to keep up with people on our street. I don't want my kids to feel inferior going to school in discount clothes." Trapped!

"I hate that we've missed church so much since we bought a boat. I want to be a good steward of my resources so since we bought the boat we have to be on the boat." Trapped!

"I think marriage would make me happy. I'm doing OK now, but if I could only get married, I would finally feel complete." Trapped!

List some examples of this kind of discontented thinking either from your own experience or someone you've observed:
"God, You've provided a job for me, but I want _____."

"God, You've provided _____ _____ for me, but I want _____."

"God, You've provided _____ for me, but I want _____."

"God, You've provided _____ for me, but I want _____."

Why do you think some of the Israelites hoarded the manna God provided? (See Ex. 16:14-20.)

Meditate on the following verses today: "A glad heart makes a cheerful face, but by sorrow of heart the spirit is crushed" (Prov. 15:13). "But you, O Lord, are a shield about me, my glory, and the lifter of my head" (Ps. 3:3). Contentment is more than just a satisfaction with material things. Contentment is a satisfied attitude about life.

Besides money, what are some other things on which you and/or other people have banked your happiness? How effective is it?

Pursuit of contentment from:	How effective is it? (circle one)		
_____	Not at all	For a time	Satisfying
_____	Not at all	For a time	Satisfying
_____	Not at all	For a time	Satisfying

According to Philippians 4:11-13, what was Paul's attitude toward the circumstances in his life?

What truth does he reveal in verse 11 about the developing contentment?

In verse 12, Paul referred to a "secret" he had learned about being content. What do you think that secret is?

Read 1 Timothy 6:6-10. What do you think is the "great gain" Paul referred to in verse 6?

Why is it so valuable?

Verse 7 provides a perspective that produces contentment. What is that perspective? Why does it help?

What are the potential consequences of discontent?

In 1 Timothy 6:17, Paul said that God provides us with everything for our enjoyment. Have you found this to be true? On what evidence do you base your answer?

What kind of provision from God do you think Paul is referring to?

Too often in our attempt to balance our cravings with a sincere desire for godliness, contentment is our canned answer. Written between the lines we communicate, "Stop complaining, stifle your craving, just resign yourself to dissatisfaction." Not true! When God says, "Be content," He means so much more. He whispers to those with willing hearts, "I am enough. Find your satisfaction in Me."

Personal Exercise

Look in a mirror. What does your face say? Are the lines in your face sketched by worry or laughter? Do your eyes twinkle, or are they sad? Is your mouth drawn tight with the pressures of life or open and ready to smile? In a private moment ask yourself if it reflects a faith and trust in God or a burdened spirit, caught up in what you strive after but never find.

"Godliness actually is a means of great gain when accompanied by contentment" (1 Tim. 6:6, NASB). Contentment has a partner. Godliness with contentment is great gain. Godliness keeps you pressing on, growing in your walk with Christ. It's refusing to be OK with where you are. Contentment, on the other hand, is being satisfied with what you have. Godliness is not content with who I am; contentment is being satisfied with what I have, satisfied with what God has provided.

Too often, however, we think we need to supplement the satisfaction equation with an *and*. Godliness and something else will make me content. Do any of these show up in your thinking?

Godliness + Prosperity = Great Gain

All I need is just more and bigger and better, and then I will be content. Contrary to a lot of errant, warped teaching in recent decades, Jesus didn't die so that you can be healthy and wealthy. Sadly, people by the thousands have bought into this heretical propaganda. Everyone wishes it were true: godliness plus prosperity equals great gain, but it's not. It's a false equation drawn from greed and self-centeredness, not God's Word.

Godliness + Poverty = Great Gain

People overreact, and the pendulum swings wide the other way: Oh, so contentment has nothing to do with having money? I guess I shouldn't have any money. I'll renounce it all. I've taken a vow of poverty. Having possessions is wrong. Godliness plus poverty must equal contentment. That incorrect equation is not taught in Scripture.

Godliness + Power + Influence = Great Gain

Some say, "Well, if it's not money, it must be power and influence." That kind of thinking has produced a generation of control freaks. Everything has to be perfect—your home, your yard, your spouse, your kids, your schedule, your income. Everything is in order. If I'm a godly person and control my own little kingdom and make everything perfect, I'll have great gain. Wrong answer. Godliness plus control plus power plus influence does not equal gain.

Godliness + Family Harmony = Great Gain

Some would die for this one. While I am all for promoting biblical principles of family living, you're never going to have a perfect family; one of your kids will make sure of that. You'll also never have a perfect marriage. Don't put all your eggs in that basket. Obey God's Word, but don't set yourself up for a lot of hurt by thinking, If I could just be a godly person and pour everything I have into my family, then I would have great gain.

Godliness + Ministry Success = Great Gain

Pour yourself into ministry, and that will deliver, some think. Wrong answer. Here's one the Lord has to teach every great-hearted servant in vocational or lay ministry: happiness is not found in successful ministry. A lot of good things happen when God's people serve Him and one another, but great gain comes only from godliness plus contentment.

Be honest. Have you been trying a false equation? Which one? Circle the false equation you most identify with. Have you judged God harshly because you have been trying an equation that doesn't work? How many frustrated prayers have you prayed, asking for success in one of these areas that you have equated with contentment? Say out loud: I've believed the wrong equation. The only true one is: Godliness with contentment is great gain.

If you are a child of God, you are called to be content with the gifts God chooses to give you. Those gifts could include material possessions, physical health, marital status, children, ministries, or whatever. No matter where you find yourself today relative to these gifts, God calls you to be satisfied.

The most tangible of these gifts is monetary so we'll begin there. Read again 1 Timothy 6:6-10.

It's been said that you'll never see a hearse towing a U-haul truck. How does verse 7 speak to the brevity of our possessions?

Why do you think people focus on accumulating material goods?

What do you think the trap is in verse 8? Give some examples of this trap from your own life experiences or from biographies, movies, or books.

Verse 10 does not say that money is intrinsically evil but that the love of money is. How can you know if you love money? What signals alert you that this is a problem?

How could the love of money draw you away from your faith (v. 10)?

In Matthew 6:19-21, Jesus explained the path to contentment.

Why did Jesus warn people not to build their treasure chest on earth?

Have you ever experienced the loss of something you treasured?

Living for my own desires over a lifetime brings far more than damage; it brings devastation. The eternal results of a lifetime living for my own desires is destruction.

What does it mean to lay up treasures in heaven? It means to use all that we have for the glory of God. It means to hold loosely the material things of life. It also means measuring life by the true riches of the kingdom and not by the false riches of this world.

What response do you feel toward these definitions? Do any of these ambitions stir you? frustrate you?

Whatever you value as most important (your treasure) is where you'll find your heart; that's what occupies the center of your personality—intellect, emotions, and will. Until Jesus is more important to you than your money, He doesn't have your heart. But when you surrender what you have to Jesus Christ as Lord, then He has you. He is now in the center.

What occupies your thoughts more than anything else? What's the first thing on your mind in the morning and the last think you think about at night?

1.

2.

3.

Jesus said that where your heart is, this is your treasure. Evaluate how this new discovery about your heart aligns with Matthew 6:19-21.

Hebrews says to keep your life free from love of money and to be content with what you have. What, then, becomes your satisfaction?

How can you identify with the prayer request in Proverbs 30:8-9? Is this a balanced perspective? Why or why not?

What wisdom do you see in these quotes from "the rich and famous"?
"I was happier as a boy working in a mechanic's shop, though we had nothing."
　　—Henry Ford

"I have made millions, but they brought me no happiness."
　　—John D. Rockefeller

"The care of millions is too great a load. There is no pleasure in it."
　　—Cornelius Vanderbilt

Read Ecclesiastes 5:13-15. How do these words compare to the other quotes of wealthy people?

> Man is born with his hands clenched; he dies with them wide open. Entering life, he desires to grasp everything; leaving the world, all he possessed has slipped away.
> —The Talmud

> I have held many things in my hands, and I have lost them all; but whatever I have placed in God's hands, that I still possess.
> —Martin Luther

Write the following questions on a sticky note and post it on top of your credit card or checkbook. Reflect on your answers before you buy anything beyond basic necessities. Why am I buying this? What need or want am I trying to meet? Am I trying to fill a deeper source of longing?

God, forgive us for our greedy, grabbing, more-for-me attitudes; and open our eyes to the rich, plentiful, joyful, abundant life of true contentment. Cause us even where we might struggle to believe that Your ways are better than ours, and renew our minds by Your truth that You and Your provisions are enough. In Jesus' name. Amen.

Here's a testimony from Tom and Sonja Steward of Long Beach, California:

We were like everyone else a couple years ago, on the fast track to success. Sonya and I had thriving careers with bright futures stretching out in front of us. We loved the Lord and thanked Him for the good life He had given us. By most everyone's yardstick, we were in a sweet spot.

Then I got sick—a debilitating, long, severe illness. When a bleak prognosis came back from doctors, we knew life was taking a turn. It became obvious that I could no longer work; and after months of feeling torn between her demanding job and caring for me, Sonya resigned from her job. I can't tell you how many sleepless nights we had. The range of our emotions swung from determination to despair. It was more than a dark night of the soul; this was our future. Gone were the days of freedom and healthy bank accounts, retirement excursions, and spending time and money on our grandchildren. Our focus became surviving the next 12 hours.

I won't tell you that there weren't moments of despair. We usually took turns. But a radical change happened on June 13, 2002—the day we got the worst news: no further treatment. Not because I was recovering—in fact, just the opposite. My wife and I got to the end of ourselves. We prayed something like this, "We have no hope except in You, Savior. We have no more strength except for what You would give us. We don't know how many days You've planned for us on this earth, Lord; but from here on out each one of them is Yours. Pour Your Spirit into us, and make us more like You. We trust You, and we thank You for opening our eyes to Your goodness and grace. We confess we didn't see it as clearly when life was on high ground. Thank You for bringing us low and removing all the distractions of life. Thank You for this disease that has opened our eyes."

We learned Paul's secret to contentment: it's through Christ. Through Christ who strengthens us. Our hearts are like wells that bubble up with gratitude for every small thing: for a day of opportunity to bring God glory with our attitude—with many more days just like it stretching in front of us, for a home where we can be together, for the sacredness of our wedding vows, in sickness and in health. For blessings like kind doctors and neighbors, patient sales clerks, loving adult children who share the load. We thank Him for good food, clean sheets, and a thoughtful church body. We linger in His Word for hours, reading and talking about new insights. We never would have taken the time for any of that before, much less have been grateful for it.

Gone is the drive to go, go, go; it's been replaced by pray, pray, pray. Life came to a screeching slowdown; and we discovered another life, a better life, underneath. We receive what He gives us, and we're thankful for it. We have enough. The words of Paul have become our witness: "Not that I am speaking of being in need, for I have learned in whatever situation I am to be content. I know how to be brought low, and I know how to abound. In any and every circumstance, I have learned the secret of facing plenty and hunger, abundance and need. I can do all things through Him who strengthens me" (Phil. 4:11-13).

> What about Tom and Sonja's testimony was notable to you? Do you believe this is truly how it is for them, or are you skeptical?

How do you explain their attitude in this trial?

Have you or someone close to you ever experienced the leveling effects of a trial?
What are key decisions you can make that will make you bitter or better?

In what ways can you follow their lead in a trial you are facing right now?

How do you see contentment and gratitude connected?

All of us have days when we don't feel particularly blessed, particularly during a trial. If that is your situation today, take heart. God's Word teaches that we are blessed in more ways than we could ever think or imagine. We just tend to get hung up on counting our troubles instead of counting our blessings. Put in the proper perspective, our problems—no matter how big they are or may seem—can even be seen as blessings. The choice is attitude.

Read Philippians 4:11-13. Verse 13 is an often-quoted verse of encouragement. Explain a fuller application of Philippians 4:13 in light of verses 11-12. How does this passage answer the question, How can I be content?

Read Philippians 2:5-8 and 2 Corinthians 8:9. What example did Jesus set as it relates to greed, status, and stuff?

In what ways has God made you rich?

When you count your blessings, begin with the spiritual blessings you have in Christ Jesus. The following verses can get you started. Feel free to add your own favorite verses to this list. Read the verse and write the spiritual blessing God has promised you in Christ. From 1 John 1:9, for example, you might write: God will forgive my sin if I confess it to Him and repent.
Psalm 103:4-5

Psalm 116:1

John 3:16

John 10:28

Hebrews 4:16

2 Peter 3:9

How do these reminders contribute to your choice of contentment?

How can you specifically demonstrate your gratitude to God in a new way?

You've read many verses of Scripture today. Choose one that the Spirit used to speak to your heart, and ponder how the Lord wants to communicate to you about His faithfulness.

Jesus talked about money more than He talked about heaven and hell put together. Scripture shows that He talked about finances all the time. Of His 38 parables, 16 are about finances and how to use them for God's blessing and how to keep them from abusing yourself and others. In the New Testament, five hundred verses teach about prayer and fewer than five hundred verses talk about faith but more than two thousand deal with financial matters.

Your attitude about your money is a big deal and one of the core issues in setting your contentment meter. This area is often the one thing that enslaves your heart when God wants to own all that you are. When you consider the choice you have to replace your covetous attitude with an attitude of contentment, do you become worried about your finances? Do you wonder whether you'll come up short if you give to God?

Today we'll look at three things Jesus said in Luke 12 about how to have an attitude of contentment. Don't just read about them and answer the questions; really consider how you can align your life with what Jesus said.

More Is Not Better

Jesus said, "A man's life does not consist in the abundance of his possessions" (v. 15, NIV). You say, "I know life isn't about stuff," but saying it and living it are different. Do you really believe what the Bible says? Or do you think that somehow more stuff is going to enhance your life?

Happier people are not necessarily people who have more. A bigger house won't make you happier. Neither will a new car, nice clothes, or exotic vacations. I've fellowshipped with people around the world who live in shelters you wouldn't store your yard ornaments in. But these people have bigger smiles, more joyful worship, and a greater sense of God's fullness than some of us have ever known! More is not better. Bigger bank accounts and emptier souls indicate that many times more is worse. That's what Jesus was saying when He talked about the danger of riches and the tendency to trust in things.

> Think back over your life. Have there been times when you had less but enjoyed life more? When? What were the contentment factors?

If My Wallet Is for Self, My Heart Is Not for God

Pull your wallet out of your pocket or purse. Hold it in your hands. Look at it. This object symbolizes all that God has given to you. Keep hold of it as you read Luke 12:31-32. This verse is the only place in Scripture where we are called "little flock." Jesus is so tender and knows we get really protective when we hold our money in our hands. He said that God wants to give you the kingdom. That's what we get—the kingdom of God! All that belongs to the Creator of the universe. How foolish we are to grip so tightly to our little smidgen of resources and in our disobedience shut ourselves off from the resources of Almighty God.

Jesus said, "Sell your possessions, and give to the needy" (v. 33). He didn't mean you should liquidate everything. If we did, we would all be on government assistance. What Jesus meant is, "Don't spend so much that you can't give."

Are there ministries you'd like to support financially but you can't because you're overcommitted in keeping up your lifestyle? What are they?

What about your church—do you faithfully give to kingdom efforts there? ☐ **Yes** ☐ **No**
Do you make excuses about why you don't give or why you don't give as much or as often as you should? If so, what excuses do you give?

If you are tithing and have money left over, is it wrong to want to buy a better car? Or a better house? ☐ **Yes** ☐ **No** ☐ **Depends**
What principle does Jesus teach in verse 34 that bears truth on this issue?

The Time to Give Is Now

The right time to give is right now. Not next year or when you have more money. Not when you get the mortgage paid down or receive a raise. The time to give is now. Jesus said, "Keep your lamps burning, and be like men who are waiting for their master to come home from the wedding feast, so that they may open the door to him at once when he comes" (vv. 35-36). In other words, always be prepared because Jesus could come back at any moment. "If he comes in the second watch, or in the third, and finds them awake, blessed are those servants!" (v. 39). Being faithful to God in money matters will result in blessings for your faithfulness.

Though I've been in ministry a long time, I've never worried about the financial needs of the kingdom. God is not up in heaven thinking, "We really need kingdom people to come through for us or we won't be able to pay these bills!" I get excited to see people experience freedom when they realize that the next thing they buy or the next vacation they take will not make them happier. Only living for and obeying Christ is going to turn that key. It is my prayer that He will give you courage to put Him first and to experience the abundant provision He promises to those who obey His Word.

Hoarding Is for Fools

In the parable beginning in verse 16, Jesus called a person a fool who hoards his income for himself and doesn't generously share it. Hear Jesus' heart in this matter. He is asking, "Why are you investing in what doesn't last?" You say, "It's complicated. What would I give up? If I gave generously, what about my kids? My retirement?" But Jesus, knowing your concerns, simplified it in the next few verses. In verses 22 and 28 He said, "Therefore I say to you, do not worry about your life, what you will eat; nor about the body, what you will put on. ... If then God so clothes the grass, which today is in the field and tomorrow is thrown into the oven, how much more will He clothe you, O you of little faith" (NKJV).

Ouch. Jesus was saying, "You must trust in Me more. If you put God first, do you think He is going to leave you behind? This whole matter of giving is about faith. You have a weekly choice at church when the offering plate goes by. You can choose to give and trust God, or you can choose to hoard and trust yourself. God has asked you to give Him 10 percent. Will you? Or will you hold on to it, doubting that God will supply? It's all a matter of faith."

Ask yourself this question, "Does everything I have belong to God?"

You'll Know You're Discontent When You …

… feel left behind. The grass always looks greener over there, wherever that may be. You doubt whether God's promised green pastures and still waters even exist (Ps. 23:2). Or maybe everyone else has gone there and left you behind in the wilderness.

… feel left out. Hey—I'm over here! Don't you want to tell me what a good job I'm doing? You'll know you're discontent when you look for strokes from those who have more, do more, and go where you can't go. You haven't yet discovered that true fellowship is a by-product of working side by side in the same kingdom project (1 Cor. 12:12-26).

… feel left over. Discontented people shudder at leftovers. You'll know you're in the wilderness of discontentment when you think you deserve better than you've got (Rom. 12:3).

You'll Know You're Content When You …

… have the right attitude. Like Paul in Philippians 4:11, you are learning to be content with what you have. You know you're content when you're thankful for what you have instead of resentful for what you don't have.

… have the right perspective. God has promised always to provide what you need (Phil. 4:19), not what you think you need. It's hard sometimes to see the difference. You'll know you're content when you focus on managing instead of accumulating (1 Cor. 4:2).

… have the right balance. You know you're content when you won't cross certain lines in your career. You won't make certain sacrifices just to move up the ladder. Your interior life is more important than what others see; family and faith are more important than fun; and memories are more important than money (Phil. 3:12-16).

You Can't Outgive God

First things belong to God. The first moments of the day are His, the first day of the week, the first of my talents, the first of my treasures, the first of my time. Not only does God deserve them, but they belong to Him. My best also belongs to God. Some people say, "I'm not a morning person. It's hard for me to spend time with the Lord so early." Then give Him your best time and focus at night. Give God your best in every area of your life—your time, talents, energy, and finances.

Many people track with this concept until they get to the last word on that list, finances. When it comes to giving generously and sacrificially to God first, they draw the line and retreat into a self-protected shell. What if I don't have enough? God knows what you give to Him. You don't need to fear coming up short at the end of the month because you gave to Him first. No, God is in debt to nobody. You can't outgive God. He will stand with those who stand with Him. You give, and God will give back to you in a thousand different ways.

You may have already tasted and seen that the Lord is good. You have proved God's faithfulness and are living under the outpourings of His blessings. Others have never tasted that sweetness because they've not yet stepped out in faith to put God first. They wonder, *Why is it always so tough for us? Why do we struggle every month? Could this be it?* You can't have victory in your finances until you first get victory in giving. You're on your own if you don't put God first.

Examine this area of your life. You're making a statement of what you believe about God every time the offering is taken. Every gift is a step of faith. Ask God to prove Himself to you and He will.

It's your turn. Give generously and sacrificially to God for a week, a month, a year; and you'll have stories of God's faithfulness to tell for the rest of your life. God can give a lot to people who are willing to give it back to Him.

God help us to live true to His Word and in the light of His promises and provision.

> Want to live a simpler, less distracted life? Choose one of the following strategies and put it in action this week.
> 1. Buy things for their usefulness rather than their status. Stop trying to impress people with your clothes, car, and homes, and impress them with your life.
> 2. Reject anything that is producing an addiction in you. Refuse to be a slave to anything but God.
> 3. Develop a habit of giving things away. Declutter. Simplify your life.
> 4. Refuse the craving for the newest and the best.
> 5. Learn to enjoy things without owning them.
> 6. Look with a healthy skepticism at all "buy now, pay later" schemes.
> 7. Keep the main thing (Matt. 6:33), the main thing. Don't let things, even good things, distract you from God's priorities.

A study of godly contentment is not a survey of how to get along with less or how to live more simply. It has nothing to do with quelling your ambition. In fact, it's the exact opposite of all those things. Contentment is all about how to live more abundantly in Christ. How to go deeper into the great things of God. How to press on with holy passion and to take hold with both hands of all that God has for you.

Contentment is actually about wanting more—more of Christ and less of everything else. It's not to roll over and sigh with resignation to be satisfied with your lot in life, but it is to sense in your Spirit all that you have in your salvation and relationship with Christ and to want more of that. A holy contentment is to want less of yourself and more of Him—more of His life in you and all the peace and passion and exhilaration of being swept up into His plans and purposes and activities in this world. This is the life abundant that He promises to those who are found in Him and draw their joy and satisfaction from an ever-deepening relationship with Him (John 10:10).

We're talking now of things beyond dollar signs and resumes—to be empty-handed before God and fall into His embrace, finding Him to be enough, more than enough. More than your imagination would ever allow or enable you to believe about Him (Eph. 3:20). Contentment says no to the clamoring voice of your flesh crying, "I want," and, "I need." It's saying no to pride and self-confidence that have made you restless and unhappy. Contentment is saying yes to the longing for God that is deep within your soul.

To want less than this is to dive headlong down the slippery slope of a lukewarm life—pursuing but never finding, striving, never resting. But when you go hard after Christ, when you zealously and single-mindedly pursue Christ to know Him and enjoy Him and trust Him, the reward is your deep joy and His great honor. This is the contented life. If this is your desire, pause now before the Lord. Make this prayer your own.

> *Lord, I want to know You and the power of Your resurrected life. I put behind me the things of this life that have distorted and distracted me from embracing all that You have for me. They are but a shadow of satisfaction compared with knowing You. I come to you now, empty-handed but with a full heart. Fill me with Your Spirit and a holy discontent with where I am with You today. I press on to know You more. My heart's desire is _____. In Jesus' name, amen.*

Philippians teaches us much about contentment. Contentment is not giving up any of your wealth (4:19), fame (2:10), position (4:1), or accomplishments (3:7). It's exchanging your wealth for for what you already have.

The Source of Joy

So how's it going with your joy? If you're thinking, Why do I see joy in other people's lives but not in my own? ask yourself some hard questions beginning with, "Why am I not content?" Originally, the Greek word for *contentment* described a country that needed no imports. They had everything they needed. They had enough.

I was in a store this week when a check-out lady asked me, "Have you got your lottery ticket yet? Thirty-three million dollars—you've got to get a ticket!"

I answered, "You know, I don't need $33 million," and she looked at me kind of funny. I explained, "It wouldn't make me any happier."

The girl beside her said, "It'd make me happier," to which I added, "Or more miserable."

Our dialogue reminded me of how many people live with all their eggs in the "more basket." "If I could just get more …" I wonder how many people are going to have to drive over the money-doesn't-make-you-happy cliff before they figure out this truth? Joy resides in contentment; it's an incredible virtue. But contentment in what exactly?

Contentment in where I am. I live in Chicago. Living in Chicago offers us some phenomenal opportunities and also some pretty aggravating situations. But I've decided that I want to pastor one church my whole life if God will allow me that privilege and the people continue to give grace. To do that means I'm periodically going to have to make some contentment choices.

Contentment in what I do. You may say, "I don't like what I do." Well, let me tell you, I don't like some of the things I do either. But we've all got to do what God has called us to do. In that choice our contentment can grow.

Contentment in what I have. At the end of the day, I'm going to be a lot happier if I just accept what I have. Psalm 62:10, NKJV, says, "If riches increase do not set your heart on them." Happiness is not in having; happiness is in contentment. "Be content with such things as you have. For He Himself has said, 'I will never leave you nor forsake you' " (Heb. 13:5, NKJV).

Contentment in who I'm with. "I wish my wife was a little more …" "If my husband would just change …" You can focus on your spouse's shortcomings and stay miserable if you want, or you can choose to concentrate on the good. "Finally … whatsoever things are true, … honest, … just, … pure, … lovely, … of good report, … think on these things" (Phil. 4:8).

Do you see? That's where the joy is. I hear you say, "I can do a couple of those, James, but I don't think I can ever be content in all these areas, all the time. I'm just not there." Here's good news. You can learn to be content (Phil. 4:11). Where do you go to sign up for that course? You're already enrolled; it's a course called life.

One of the primary lessons God teaches in this course is, as Paul described, "I know how to be brought low" (Phil. 4:12). He takes things away from you, and He finds out how little you can really be satisfied with. Is God bringing you low right now? He's trying to teach you something—something that will bring a lot of joy into your life. Instead of resisting the hard stuff, why don't you get low as fast as you can? The word used for "to be brought low" is the same word in Philippians 2:8 that says Jesus humbled Himself. Don't you want to go where Jesus went? Don't fight it or blame others or deny it; accelerate what God wants you to learn by humbling yourself under it. Embrace it.

Here's the second lesson: I know how to abound. The word *abound* means "excess, overflow." Wealth has destroyed more character than poverty. More people have been ruined by having too much than by having too little. Psalm 62:10, NASB, says, "If riches increase, do not set your heart upon them." Can God trust you with a lot?

Before he closes Philippians, Paul let us in on a huge secret. "I have learned the secret of facing plenty and hunger, abundance and need, I can do all things through him who strengthens me" (Phil. 4:12-13). The Christian life is Jesus living His life through me. Underline this verse in your Bible.

You can be content when God brings you low; you can be content when the abundance overflows. You cannot get overly discouraged in the lack. You cannot get overly inflated in the abundance. You can be steady and strong and choose joy in every circumstance. There's no mystery about it. The secret of being content is this: "I have learned in whatsoever state I am to be content. ... I can do those things through him who strengthens me" (Phil. 4:11,13).

Where are you in God's school of contentment? Have you graduated from the "brought low" course? from the "abound" course? Is God free to bring you low and humble you? Will you still love and trust Him? Do you still walk with Him in the land of blessing? Discuss this with a close friend.

Are you discontent because you are cut off from the source of your joy? If you've worked through this entire week's study and you're left feeling dull or cynical or wishing things were different in your heart, perhaps it's time to return to the Lord and ask Him to probe your heart. Consider the following questions and reflect or write a prayer on the lines below.

Do you have sin you need to confess? ☐ Yes ☐ No

Are you thinking more highly of yourself than you ought? ☐ Yes ☐ No

Have you been investing time in your relationship with God and allowed for Him to fill your cup?
☐ Yes ☐ No

Where has your focus been lately?

What God Is Showing Me

In this lesson, I've learned that contentment is satisfaction in _____.

Godliness + anything other than contentment will not add up to great gain. Not
_____ or _____ or _____ or
_____.

When I choose gratitude for all God has given me rather than resentment for what He hasn't, I am cultivating a great atmosphere of

When I am generous, I communicate to God and others that

According to Philippians 4:11, the secret of being content is

My choice today, based on what I've learned this week, is to

REPLACE A CRITICAL ATTITUDE ...

Group Activity

In small groups of five, ask participants to share responses to this question: What temptations have you faced this week in the area of money and possessions? Give one another the opportunity to respond and offer loving, mutual accountability.

1. How content are you?

2. How can you learn to be content with what God has provided?

3. How are gratitude and contentment linked?

4. How are generosity and contentment linked?

5. What is the source of true, lasting contentment?

Discussion Questions
About Contentment

Video

We are back in the desert looking at a critical attitude. Are you a critical person? Watch. Listen. Apply biblical truths to your own situation.

Video Notes

Criticism—To dwell on the perceived _**faults**_ of another person with no view to their good.

Criticism is _**wrong**_.

Criticism ruins our _**fellowship**_ with God.

Criticism is _**wrong**_ for our relationship with others.

Criticism is wrong for us _**personally**_.

Every time God says, "Don't," what He means is, "Don't _**hurt**_ yourself."

Criticism is _petty_.

Sometimes the real issue is _unforgiveness_

Sometimes the real issue is _envy_ or jealousy.

Sometimes the real issue is personal _failure_.

Criticism is self-_exalting_.

Every time I throw _dirt_ I lose ground.

Criticism is _painful_

Criticism is often _inadvertent_.

Criticism plugs the flow of God's _blessings_ into our lives.

1. Think about someone you know who is critical. What do you think the real issue is for this person?

2. What was the real issue when Aaron and Miriam were critical of Moses? _envy, jealousy_

3. Why is criticism so often a part of family relationships?

4. Share a time when you have seen a relationship ruined by criticism.

5. When, if ever, is criticism helpful?

Discussion Questions
About a Critical Attitude

Study **Challenge**

Do you have a critical attitude? This week's study will take a look at contemporary situations and biblical truths to help you assess whether you need to change your critical attitude.

Memory Verse

"Let no corrupting talk come out of your mouths, but only such as is good for building up, as fits the occasion, that it may give grace to those who hear. And do not grieve the Holy Spirit of God, by whom you were sealed for the day of redemption. Let all bitterness and wrath and anger and clamor and slander be put away from you, along with all malice. Be kind to one another, tenderhearted, forgiving one another, as God in Christ forgave you."
Ephesians 4:29-32

Few things put you in the wilderness faster than a critical attitude. This attitude saps all the joy out of your relationships and sends your own perspective to a dry land far from promised-land living. All of us at one level or another struggle with a critical attitude. The root of our thinking is much deeper than being overanalytical or overopinionated. While it may have started with hearing others talk down other people, it continues by choice. It has to do with all of the games we play to get people to do what we want them to do, hopefully without their knowing we're trying to do it.

Like a slow poison, we may experience the consequences of a critical attitude without realizing it. Everything God says is wrong is something that is injurious to us. When God says, "Don't criticize," it's not because He is trying to deprive us of some satisfactory experience but rather to protect us from destructive consequences. Being critical goes against the nature of who He created you to be. Fish were made to swim. Birds were made to fly. People were made to live in fellowship with God. When we sin, we break our fellowship with God. We hinder our human happiness, and life becomes like a wilderness. That's why God says, "Don't do it." He has some strong feelings about our negative, critical patterns of thinking.

Caution: this lesson is going to be convicting. Start praying right now.

Let's start with a definition and then break it down. Criticism—To dwell on the perceived faults of another with no view to their good.

Perceived. The reason we should say *perceived* faults is because everything you might think is wrong with someone is not necessarily wrong. You may be unaware of certain circumstances, or the problem may be with you. If you're going to get victory over a critical attitude, you have to get past am-I-right or am-I-wrong thinking. A negative, critical attitude is destructive even when the faults are only perceived.

To dwell upon the perceived faults of another. That's the key issue. You'll find two kinds of people in this area, encouragers and analyzers. Analytical thinkers march through life and continually scrutinize. Why did they do that? Why is that there? Someone should have taken care of that. If you think that way, you have an extra challenge to see something that's not right and not to run over it and over it in your mind.

If you're an analytical person, a lot of data comes across your circuits. You can't necessarily stop that since God made you that way. However, you can choose not to dwell on it. You might say, "But how can you help a person if you don't dwell on what you see?" Great question. That's why I added that last part.

With no view to their good. A critical person just stirs the pot. A person who sees the error and wants to do good can do two things. First, if you observe a brother or sister who is struggling in a certain area, it's not a negative, critical attitude to dwell upon it if that prompts you to go before the Lord on their behalf and ask God to help that person.

You can take it one more step. You can go to the person. If you know and you care about the one you've observed, it's not a critical attitude to focus on your observation and say, "Can I talk to you about something a little sensitive? I care about you and want you to know I would only bring this up if I thought it would help you. You probably aren't aware that you …"

Are you an analytical thinker who gets carried away into criticism? ☐ Yes ☐ No

Have you ever had the embarrassing experience of unjustly criticizing (inwardly or outwardly) someone and then learned later that what you thought was true was not? What did you learn from that?

In your mind, what's the difference between exhorting people toward good and criticizing them for what they're doing?

How can you test your thinking to discern if you are critiquing for good or criticizing?

Are you quick to find fault? ☐ Yes ☐ No If you are, confess this as sin.

Read Numbers 12 in your Bible and answer the following questions.

Who was criticized for what and by whom in this passage?
Who _____ For what _____ By whom _____ _____

What did their statement reveal about their criticism?

Moses was likely used to being criticized. Why do you think this situation was harder to take?

What did God say to Miriam and Aaron about this criticism?

What did God do to punish Miriam?

Do you think it too harsh? ☐ Yes ☐ No Why?

Don't be too hard on Miriam. Miriam wasn't an ungodly woman. She loved Moses. She saved his life when he was a baby by hiding him in the bulrushes. She arranged for him to be nursed by their mother even when he was with Pharaoh's daughter in the palace. And when they crossed the Red Sea, Miriam wrote the worship song to celebrate that great victory. You can read the lyrics in Exodus 15. She was a righteous woman, which tells you that you don't want to think you're so far along spiritually that you might not struggle with a critical attitude. Nobody can say, "That sin is so behind me!" or, "That'll never be an issue for me." Potentially everyone could struggle with a critical attitude. Certainly that was true of Miriam.

Case Study: The Damage Was Done

A group of friends from a former job met for dinner, and the name of a mutual acquaintance came up. He had recently released his second book. I had read his latest book and found it disappointing. Instead of saying that I thought his first book had been better, I ranted that he was a one-book wonder and that his second book was shallow. Suddenly I stopped myself, realizing how unkind and unnecessary my comments were. I stumbled through some words of praise and apologized for my negative attitude. But it was too late; I had already damaged the reputation of a brother in Christ, and I can never take back my words.

> Have you ever felt convicted by a random, hurtful word coming out of your mouth? Describe it. How quickly did you feel the Spirit's prompt?

Meditate on Psalm 19:14 today: "Let the words of my mouth and the meditation of my heart be acceptable in your sight, O Lord, my rock and my redeemer."

Personal Exercise

For the entire day tomorrow, pretend that every word you speak is being captured on a hidden tape recorder and will be played back in public. Ask the Lord to show you your critical spirit.

Be grateful for the deep emotion that conviction stirs in your heart. That means the Spirit is at work in you, revealing the things that grieve the Lord. Remember that pain and resolve to hate the sin of criticism with a new vengeance.

We've been looking at the account of Miriam and Aaron criticizing their brother Moses. Review Numbers 12:1: "Then Miriam and Aaron spoke against Moses because of the Cushite woman." Apparently Moses' first wife Zipporah, a Midianite, had died; and Moses had chosen another woman to marry. And guess what? Big sister didn't like the new choice. But is that really what all the petty criticism was about? Verse 2 (NASB) reveals a deeper problem: "They said, 'Has the Lord indeed spoken only through Moses? Has He not spoken through us as well?' " Moses' wife was the surface issue. The real problem was their jealousy of Moses' prominence. How come Moses gets all the attention? We're leading too! Everyone loves Moses. "Moses this" and "Moses that." We're so sick of hearing Moses' name. What about me? What about my role?

Then verse 3 clarifies the real issue. "Now the man Moses was very humble, more than any man who was on the face of the earth" (NASB). Moses flat out didn't deserve their sharp words, and God stepped in for his defense. "And the Lord heard [their criticism]. … And the anger of the Lord was kindled against them, and he departed" (vv. 2,9).

Criticism is the disapproval of people, not for having faults, but having faults different from your own.

We'll skip a lot of the petty reasons we criticize and go for radical, invasive heart surgery. You might want to take a deep breath.

Lord, my natural tendency is to rationalize and excuse my critical attitude, and then nothing ever changes, and I wonder why. Help me be different today. If I pretend there's nothing wrong, I'll die a slow and painful death. So open my eyes to see the things in my heart that keep your grace from overflowing in my life. Do the surgery; get all the cancer out. I choose life today, life in Your Spirit. You are so kind and merciful to linger over me right now. I die to my pride and embrace Your life in me. Amen.

Get to the Real Issue

As a pastor, I've sat in a lot of marriage counseling sessions. That's where you hear prime examples of cloaked issues. Question: Why are you struggling in your marriage? Answers: "He doesn't like my parents." "She loses my socks." "He travels too much." "She doesn't keep the house picked up." So you probe for the real issue. Why? What's behind that? If you want to get forward in that relationship, you've got to get past the criticism to the deeper issue.

If you have ever had somebody criticize you about some incidental thing you do and then you deal with it, what do you find out? As soon as you solve that problem, they're on to something else. The petty criticism is a covering for a real heart issue.

Well, What Are Those Issues?

1. **Unforgivingness.** Unforgivingness fuels criticism. I was talking a while ago with a godly, dear woman who loves the Lord. All of a sudden the subject of her former son-in-law came up. This sweet-spirited lady, who just a moment ago had been discussing the things of God, said, "He's a jerk! I hate him!" Obviously a lot of hurt had come from that relationship, but her criticism was just a covering for an unforgiving heart.

Have you ever wondered why you can tolerate, even excuse, some irritating behavior in some people; but when someone with whom you have an unresolved issue does the same behavior, you jump all over them?

☐ **Yes** I've done that. ☐ **No** I don't know what you're talking about.

Why do you think this is?

When unforgivingness is in the heart, criticism will be on the lips.

On what condition does Colossians 3:13 plead with us to forgive those who have hurt us?

2. **Bitterness.** The root of bitterness is the pain of heart caused by living apart from God's grace. It's the wounded, unattended, infected, foul-smelling heart that refuses to do things God's way. As a root bitterness usually grows beneath the surface; it's inside you. Nobody can see it, but before long it squirms its way around your heart and strangles your love for God, your victory, and your joy. All the good things in the Christian life go sour because you're not submitting to God's Spirit.

Why does bitterness belong in the Ephesians 4:31 list?

More Issues That Prompt a Critical Spirit:
Anger
Irritation
Disappointment
Unmet Expectations
Impatience
Stress
Guilt

3. **Envy and Resentment.** Many times people are critical because they are jealous of someone's success, and they try to pull that person down to their level. Some people who live in defeat become critical of others because they're discouraged about their own lives and their failure before the Lord. They want to level the playing field. Yeah, maybe I'm struggling, but he's not perfect either. How petty.

How does Proverbs 14:30 summarize the fruit of envy?

4. **Careless, Thoughtless Words.** Many of the critical things we say are just careless words, not ready-aim-fire intentional injury but loose lips. Things spill out of our mouths that on a better day, when we are filled with the Spirit and focused on what's right, we would never choose to say. Criticism is often unintentional. By our dumb carelessness we damage ourselves and others.

How did Aaron describe their criticism in Numbers 12:11?

What does his quick realization say about his heart?

What does 2 Corinthians 10:5 tell us to do to guard against these harmful, inadvertent words?

5. Pride. Talk about the root of the problem! Criticism is really self-exalting. Criticism is ultimately putting yourself higher and the other person lower. It takes the focus off your faults and elevates you as the one who discerns right and wrong, good and bad. Anything that makes you feel bigger is not conducive to your spiritual life. Criticism also cloaks insecurity. A critic says subconsciously, "If I can't make my mark in this world by what I do, maybe I'll make it for knowing what others need to do better." God will not honor that kind of thinking.

> Beware of anything that puts you in the place of the superior person.
> —Oswald Chambers

With what phrase does Romans 12:3 describe the way we ought to think about ourselves?

Take It Personally.

Do you see yourself in any of the "real issue" descriptions? If so, which one?

> The critic constantly looks at a situation from the human point of view. Their opinion. Their procedure. Their arrangement. They know 17 reasons something will not work, but they cannot come up with a better plan to see that the job gets done. They see everything from their own point of view and don't realize that something's going on in each of our lives and in the circumstances of life that is purely God's work.

Hint: If you don't identify with any of these, you need to ask the Lord to show you and be open to what He says. Spend some time today, praying for your own heart as it relates to the deeper issues of criticism.

Nothing spreads like a virus through a family or a local church, a student body, a business, a staff, or an organization more than a negative, petty, critical spirit. Where does all that come from? Why do we so often end up saying such critical, hurtful words? Have you ever asked yourself, "Why do I …

… bring to the surface and dwell on someone's faults?"

… grumble bitterly over someone's minor annoyances?"

… spit out words intended to wound the people I love?"

Criticism leads to discontentment. When you're done finding fault in every situation, you're going to be dissatisfied with your God-given lot in life.

We know in our hearts that this type of communication is caustic and sinful. So why do fall into the trap again and again? James, Jesus' half-brother and writer of the New Testament letter, wrote, "No human being can tame the tongue. It is a restless evil, full of deadly poison" (Jas. 3:8). But the tongue is the fruit of the problem. Jesus got to the root of the problem in Luke 6:43-45 and answered why the best intentions to say good and helpful things often fail.

No wonder our sorry attempts at conquering a critical spirit are so worthless. We can't conquer a spiritual problem just by trying to suppress it; we will always have more ugly attitudes. We've got to get to the root. The problem is not with our mouths; it's with our hearts. Today we're going into heart surgery to determine what causes our critical attitude.

As we begin, read and meditate on these verses: Ephesians 4:31; James 4:11-12; Psalm 19:14.

Case Study in a Critical Attitude: Looking Below the Surface

After listening to the message, "Replace a Critical Attitude," I was so convicted about the way that I, a leader in our singles ministry at church, have infested our gathering with a negative attitude. Just last week my friends and I could have been overheard saying:

"Can you believe how relationally handicapped the people are who come on Thursday night?"

"Yeah, I wonder if any of them had one decent conversation this week."

"And that one group of girls! I mean, no wonder they're still single! Have they even tried Weight Watchers®?"

"Well, the guys are no different—the way they demand a girl to have the body of a supermodel but a heart for ministry like Mother Teresa. Come on! Have they looked in the mirror lately? I mean, how far can a comb-over go?"

"All I can say is their little mixers and ice breakers aren't going to solve those people's problems. I say next week we try the singles group at the church down the road."

"I'd love to join you guys, but I'm a small group leader in this crazy, dysfunctional group. I'm leading our discussion on 'Giving Grace' next week."

When I remember how we talked about our singles' group and some of the people in it, I feel grieved. I realize now how much these conversations must have saddened God. I don't think any gag order to "stop being so critical" will solve our problem. Critical words spring from critical spirits, and we all need a heart makeover.

How does this scenario illustrate that this group's critical spirit is the fruit of these spiritual issues?

Pride

Self-centeredness

Lack of love

Lack of grace

If you have an evaluative bent, you can spot flaws in people and in how things are done. It's not wrong to notice the areas where people can grow and dynamics can improve; but if you have a humble, loving heart, you would have a decidedly different pattern in dealing with those shortcomings. You would pray for the people who frustrate you and aggressively encourage them. If your heart is pure, your words can better reflect God's pattern (who, by the way, has good cause to criticize you but who loves and trains you instead.)

Look for the Source

In what situations does your spirit become critical rather than cooperative and compassionate? Be specific.

Work

Home

Church

Other

Pause and Reflect

• If you criticize people in leadership or who are known for their success, you must confess that your attitude flows from a restless heart that isn't at peace with God's plan for your life.
• If you criticize someone's skills, you must confess your ingratitude for the toolbox of resources He's given you to serve Him.
• If you mercilessly criticize people close to you for the smallest of thing, you must confess your lack of faith in God to change them (and you!).

- If you angrily broadcast the sins of people who have wronged you, you must confess your unforgivingness.
- If your speech centers on yourself or if you're prone to angry words, you must confess your lack of love.

Who is often at the center of your negative, critical attitude?
Write their names here

Ask the Spirit to reveal to you your chronic heart condition that fuels your negative attitude toward others. Check the ones His Spirit is highlighting for you.

- ☐ Lack of peace
- ☐ Lack of humility
- ☐ Lack of patience
- ☐ Lack of faith
- ☐ Lack of grace
- ☐ Lack of love
- ☐ Lack of forgiveness
- ☐ Lack of kindness
- ☐ Other: _____

When you realize you've sinned in your critical attitude, go immediately to God. Go the first time you feel convicted. Be specific about your sin and broken by its severity. Turn to Him in sincere repentance, and you can know by faith the reality of His forgiveness, mercy, and grace. This could be your moment right now. Do you need to talk to the Lord about anything right now that His Spirit has stirred in you?

WEEK 5. DAY 4. CONSEQUENCES OF A CRITICAL SPIRIT

When Jacques Plante, the great NHL goalie, retired, someone asked him how he had liked being a goalie. He quipped, "How would you like a job where if you make a mistake, a big red light goes on and 18,000 people boo?" Sadly, families can be like that. Churches and communities can be, too. And they pass on these traits from generation to generation. Have you seen that in your own family? your own church? It's time to break the cycle.

When I'm preaching, I sometimes ask people to close their eyes so that each person feels like just the two of us are in the room. They can be more honest with themselves that way. I would ask you to do that right now if you could and still keep reading; but instead, just imagine that situation for a few moments. Listen, is this week's lesson for you? All of us to some degree in our sinful, human nature want to find a way to put others down and ourselves up. Has criticism become a chronic problem, a natural way of life for you? If I asked your family and close friends, what would they say? What is the Spirit whispering to you right now?

As your brother in the Lord, I need to warn you that if you are given to criticism, something's wrong. I'm not saying that all of your opinions are wrong, nor am I saying that God doesn't love you and cannot use your life. But it's time to stop. Not only is your criticism hurtful to others, but it's eating you away on the inside. It's also driving a wedge between you and God that is not budging until you deal with this sin in God's way. And you know that all the positive thinking in the world isn't going to break this sinful bent. You need a supernatural transformation to conquer this wilderness attitude. It's long overdue, but are you ready to rid your life of this poison?

Pause right now and echo David's prayer from Psalm 139:23-24.

Ask yourself: "Why do I criticize so much? Why am I so negative, so caustic, so pessimistic? Why am I satisfied to live a life in the narrow, gray twilight of this negative attitude?"

Some wives reading this have a terribly critical attitude toward their husbands. It's ripping your home apart. Some husbands are negative toward their families. Your first reaction to anything is no. The most critical person in any church can't hold a candle to some pastors and ministry leaders who brutalize the flock of God with their criticism. Students, if you are feeding your critical spirit, you are destroying the unity of your school or dorm or youth group. Some hardworking people waste a lot of time at work, damaging others' morale.

When you choose to live this way, you are living outside of God's will for you. He intended you to know so much more joy, fulfillment, and peace than you have right now, trapped in this negative attitude. He wants to start setting you free today.

OK, open your eyes. Now open your heart.

The Consequences of a Critical Spirit

What does a critical attitude cost you and the body of Christ?

1. Disunity in the Body of Christ

What does Proverbs 6:16-19 say is the seventh thing that is "an abomination" to the Lord?

First Corinthians 12:12-31 describes the body of Christ as a single unit in cooperative harmony.

What is the consequence of criticism in this picture?

2. Divide and Conquer

The enemy of our soul has a military strategy to divide the body of Christ and undermine our joy, usefulness, and unity.

From the context what do you think could have been happening in Ephesians 4:29?

in Philippians 4:2-3?

3. Discontentment

Read Philippians 4:8-9. If you were dealing with a critical spirit, what would be the opposite things you would think about?

Instead of true

Instead of honorable

Instead of pure

Instead of lovely

Instead of commendable

Instead of excellent

Instead of worthy of praise

Criticism leads to discontent. When you're done finding fault in every situation, you're going to be dissatisfied with your God-given lot in life. Are you struggling with a critical attitude in any of the above situations? Are you experiencing a lack of joy? Could this be the cause?

4. Desensitized to the Sin of Criticism

"Well, it's the truth, isn't it?" "Let me share this with you so we can pray more intelligently." "I heard this from a reliable source, or I wouldn't be repeating it."

When you allow a critical tongue to take over, you need to bring your words and attitudes under the control of the Holy Spirit.

Read James 3:2-8 to be reminded why a controlled tongue is the mark of a mature Christian.

5. Criticism Plugs the Flow of God's Blessing

Criticism makes you hard, vindictive, and cruel. It leaves you with the prideful notion that you are a superior person. It is impossible to grow to be more like Christ and at the same time maintain a critical attitude. Oswald Chambers said, "Whenever you are in a critical temper, it is impossible to enter into communion with God."

Do you agree or disagree? ☐ **Yes** ☐ **No** Why?

How to Take Criticism—Moses' Example

If you're interested in serving people in the Lord's work, you need to know up front that you will be criticized by the very ones who will later need your help. You will need God's grace to be merciful to those who attacked you, but you must show mercy.

At one point on the 40-year wandering trek across the desert, the people wanted to kill Moses and Aaron. Just before the stones began to fly, Numbers 14:10-12 says that God showed up and offered to take care of the problem for Moses by taking Israel out permanently.

But what did Moses do? He interceded for those criticizing, dumb, rebellious people! Moses asked God to forgive Israel and reminded Him of His compassion. Did God need the reminder? No. But Moses needed the reaffirmation of his faith to remind God that he trusted God's nature. What happened? God didn't annihilate the people, but He only allowed Joshua and Caleb—two in that huge generation—to enter the promised land.

To know God's standard, first spend some time meditating on the following verses from the quote book of all ages, God's Word. What's the wisdom or encouragement in:

Proverbs 10:19

Proverbs 11:12

Proverbs 12:18

Ephesians 4:29

Philippians 2:3

Quotable Quips on Criticism

"To belittle is to be little."

"It is only imperfection that complains of what is imperfect. The more perfect we are, the more gentle and quiet we become towards the defects of others."
—Joseph Addison

"Any hack can tear down, it takes a real artist to build up."

"You will never see a monument erected to a critic."

Evaluate these secular quotes on a critical attitude as they compare with Scripture.

The proof of faith is not in the knowing but in the doing. Refresh your memory concerning what you have learned about a critical attitude:

    1. Name three evidences of a critical attitude.

    2. Name three heart issues that lead to a critical attitude.

    3. Name three consequences of a critical attitude.

Can you spot these in your real life? Read the following five case studies and answer the related questions. Flip through previous pages in this study for your answers and have your Bible handy. Ask God to reveal your critical attitude as you read.

Case Study 1. Conviction

Several friends and I were discussing major changes in my former ministry. I made a derogatory comment about a ministry leader. Suddenly I felt a lurch in my spirit as if something inside me had been ripped away. I knew I'd offended the Spirit and that He had withdrawn to some far-off corner of my heart. I had grieved the Spirit in the past, but the intensity of my remorse was new to me. I was sickened by my words, horrified by my arrogance, and saddened that I had hurt the One I loved.

    What just happened here?

    Why do you think God's Spirit was so definitive and tangible?

    What good came out of this experience for this person?

    Looking over this week's study, or from your own experience in Scripture, cite a Scripture verse that explains this case study.

    Have you ever had an experience like this? Describe it here.

Case Study 2. Overheard

You're sitting in church in front of two women. When one of the pastors and family were called to the front, you can't help overhear their comment. The pastor's wife became the target.

"Just look at her. That outfit is so scanty. You can tell what she thinks of herself. Humph!"

"Or what she thinks of her husband and his ministry! She is a stumbling block to these young Christians, not to mention the poor men in our church who need to look the other way. Why doesn't someone tell her to put on a sweater?"

    What consequence has this critical attitude yielded in the church?
    with these women? with the pastor's wife?

What should you do when correction or exhortation is appropriate? What's the difference between that and criticism?

Cite a Scripture verse that explains this case study.

Have you ever been in a situation like this? What did you do? Have you ever overheard a conversation like this? What did you do or wish to do?

Case Study 3. Victory

Since I've been in this study, I've asked the Lord to put a guard on my lips. I've prayed Psalm 39:1, "I will guard my ways, that I may not sin with my tongue; I will guard my mouth with a muzzle." I've been doing OK, but the real test came last weekend when I spent the day with a close friend. As I drove to meet her, I asked God to help me to encourage her and not to be critical in any way all day.

God answered! As we hiked along a forest path, we talked at length about my friend's frustration with her new job. As we began to discuss deeper issues, I listened and empathized with her feelings, but I also felt led to ask some hard questions and to challenge some of her perspectives. She told me later that the Spirit had spoken truth to her through several things I'd said. In turn, when I talked about a situation that had upset me, she listened lovingly but also challenged me to think a different way. All this without one word of criticism. There had been times in the past when we had gossiped and criticized others. No man (or woman) can tame the tongue, but God can!

Can you identify with this victory?

What important lesson was learned?

What heart issue prompted this change?

Cite a Scripture verse that explains this case study.

Experiment with this choice of attitude this week. When you find yourself in a situation where you have been known to feed your critical attitude, surrender it to God. Ask Him to keep your focus on positive, encouraging speech. Ask someone to pray for you in this challenge. Report when you have victory.

Case Study 4. Slander

Years ago when I was still in seminary, I remember criticizing a chapel speaker. Nobody could deny that he did a poor job preaching. In fact, my friends and I stood around afterward and discussed all the negative elements of his sermon. Just then another student walked by, someone I deeply respected for his relationship with the Lord. He grabbed my arm and pushed me aside for a private word. He said, "Man, you just don't know all the facts. Two hours ago his wife called to tell him that his youngest son had been killed. He can't get a flight home until this afternoon so he decided to stay and speak. Man, you just need to be quiet."

What just happened here?

What important lesson was learned?

What heart issue prompted this criticism? What was done wrong in this scenario, and what was done right?

What consequence came as a result of this criticism?

Cite a Scripture verse that explains this case study.

Have you ever been in a situation like this? What did you do? Have you ever overheard a conversation like this? What did you do or wish to do?

Case Study 5. Influence

An older man in our church had a grown, happy family with children who are committed to Christ and growing in their faith. What was the secret to the spiritual maturity of his children? He said: "My wife and I covenanted that our children would never hear us criticize church leaders or another brother or sister in Christ. We understood that criticism of our fellow believers was a reflection on the Lord. Why would they want to commit their lives to the One whom their parents criticized? We had left a dysfunctional church when our children were small. In our frustrated efforts to be positive change agents in that church, we said some things at home that ought not to have been said. Out of our own hurt, we caused damage in others. Shortly after coming here, we contacted those we hurt and asked their forgiveness. We also asked God to fill us with His power never to be like that again. We don't want to injure the church, nor do we want to injure our kids spiritually, even inadvertently. God has honored that request in our family's lives."

What important lesson was learned?

What heart issue prompted this scenario?

What was done wrong in this scenario and what was done right?

What positive result came from this scenario? What does this say about our influence on others? the power of our words? attitude?

Cite a Scripture verse that explains this case study.

Have you ever been in a situation where you needed to make something right or ask forgiveness for something critical that did no good? Describe it.

What God Is Showing Me

1. In this lesson I've learned that criticism is sin.
2. God cares about how we treat one another and holds accountable one who criticizes His children.
3. The root of a critical attitude is a sinful heart.
4. Criticism breeds consequence.

The lesson I want to remember from this chapter is ...

What is my choice today based on what I've learned this week?

Now Lord, under Your Spirit, I face the awesome responsibility of applying what I have studied. I am in the process of growing and becoming more like You. Thank You for Your Word that has shone into my heart. Forgive me for thinking so highly of myself. Forgive me for the arrogant thinking that my perspective is the right one. Give me grace, love, and forbearance for others. Draw to my attention and make me quick to turn from criticism that I might know Your fullness in my life. In Jesus' precious name, amen.

WITH

LOVE

Discuss in small groups: Has there ever been a time when criticism helped you? Describe how.

What temptations have you faced this week in terms of what spirit comes out of your mouths? Give one another the opportunity to respond and offer loving, helpful accountability.

1. How do you know your attitude is critical and not constructive?

2. What are the real issues behind a critical attitude?

3. What are the spiritual issues surrounding a critical attitude and a critical tongue?

4. What are the long-term consequences that result from a critical attitude?

5. How can you identify a critical attitude, its causes and results, when you hear it?

1 Cor. 13
* John 15:13

Discussion Questions
About a Critical Attitude

Video

Move away from the desert now with an attitude of love. Watch and listen for how you can change your attitude from being critical of others to loving them.

Video Notes

All truth and no __love__ is brutality.   1 Cor. 13:1-2

Agape love is __you__ before me. (selfless love)

All love and no __truth__ is hypocrisy.

On the Majors— __Action__ — You must take action

Sin   1 Cor 13:4-6
Rom 3:23
Isaiah 53:6

What is a major?

1. Is it critical _path_ ? Major fall out or doctrinal issue

2. Is it a chronic _problem_ ? Many, many times

3. Is it close _proximity_ ? (Relationship)

On the Minors— _Acceptance_ (Cultural Difference)
Personal Prefences
In All Things— _LOVE_ Personality   There is no place for
                                         ∨

I John 4:7-8   1 Cor. 13:4-5
I John 4:16

1. What Scripture passage best expresses love to you?

2. Explain why you agree or disagree with this statement: All truth and no love is brutality.

3. James MacDonald says, "Agape love is you before me." What are some real-life examples?

4. Explain why you agree or disagree with this statement: All love and no truth is hypocrisy.

5. How do you determine "majors" from "minors"?

Discussion Questions
About a Loving Attitude

Study Challenge

Do you have a loving attitude? Would you like to grow in moving from criticism to love in your relationships? This week's study will take a look at relevant Scripture passages and help you apply biblical truths to your life to move toward having a more loving attitude.

Memory Verse

"In this is love, not that we have loved God but that he loved us and sent his Son to be the propitiation for our sins. Beloved, if God so loved us, we also ought to love one another."
1 John 4:10-11

Last week we talked about putting off a critical, negative, faultfinding attitude toward others. There's no way in the world we're going to be able to put that off unless we replace it with something. What really displaces a critical attitude? The answer is an attitude of love.

If you tend to criticize some people in your life, you probably read that and thought, *If you knew my husband/wife, my boss, or my neighbor, you wouldn't ask me to do that.*

Is someone in your life hard to love? ☐ Yes ☐ No

Get some of these people's faces in your mind right now. Pause and express to God your willingness to change your attitude toward them. Determine right now that you are willing for God's Spirit to show you how to change a faultfinding, critical attitude toward them into an attitude of love. If you want out of the wilderness, this is the way.

Our study this week has great power because we're going to look hard at God's Word and determine to obey what it says. Our goal is to live out our new understanding of how to love a person and how to get victory over a critical, negative kind of attitude. Jesus said in John 13:35 that this attitude of love for one another is the number one mark of authentic Christianity. "By this all people will know that you are my disciples, if you have love for one another" (John 13:35).

When real people see the contrast between a life focused on self versus a life dedicated to loving others, it grabs their attention. Most long to know how real love by real people really works.

As we dive into our study, I want to encourage you with these two reminders:

1. If you want to grow in your ability to love others, you've got to grow in your relationship with God. You'll learn today that love is rooted in His character. His conduct flows out of His character because God is love, because God loves. A commitment to loving God will send ripple effects to your other relationships. The closer you walk with God, the more His Spirit will give you the power to love others as God loves them.

2. Loving others is a debt. Because God loves us, we ought to love one another (1 John 4:11). The message of Christianity is that God doesn't love us because we first loved Him. But by grace He chose to love us first. Because the love of God has been showered upon us, we have an obligation to love others with that same grace. We can't hoard God's love, which we did nothing to deserve. We express our gratitude by passing it on.

Since I was a small boy, I can remember singing, "Jesus loves me! this I know, for the Bible tells me so." Do you know the song? Do you also know that Jesus loves you? Have you tasted God's love? Have you experienced God's love for you personally? It's an impossible assignment to replace a critical attitude with an attitude of love if you've never experienced His love personally.

The only attitude big enough to replace a critical attitude is an attitude of love.

Only recently in my life have I known in my heart that God loves me. I'm a little embarrassed to admit this. I mean, why does a 40-something-year-old man need to know that God loves him? That's for kids, right? How stunned I was not long ago to have God meet me in such a powerful, personal way and immerse me in this idea that He loves me! I came to experience and taste His love—to know, not just with my head but with my heart, that God loves me. God truly loves you, too!

Have there been times in your life when you doubted if God really does love you? Perhaps you were going through a season of training and trials. Or perhaps your relationship with God was blocked by unconfessed sin and God seemed far away.

How were your feelings changed by your faith?

How did that season end? Or do you still feel that way?

How does God love you? Let's count the ways.

Psalm 56:8 says He loves you so much that He

Isaiah 49:16 says He loves you so much that He

Jeremiah 31:3 says He loves you so much that He

Matthew 10:30 says He loves you so much that He

This message of love is personal. It doesn't matter where you've been, what you've done, or what you've experienced; God loves you. It doesn't matter what you have thought about yourself or what other people may have said about you; God loves you. This is what God says about you! You are honored, you are precious in His eyes, and He loves you! (Isa. 43:4). Isn't that wonderful?

Most often when the Bible attempts to express God's love, it makes a beeline for the cross of Jesus Christ. The cross is God's statement about how much He loves you. When you think of the immensity of God's love, the first thing the Bible often asks you to do is to consider the price that was paid. "This is love: not that we loved God, but that he loved us and sent his Son as an atoning sacrifice for our sins" (1 John 4:10, NIV).

What makes this love so amazing is that it is highlighted against the backdrop of a debt each one of us owes. At the core of God's being is His holiness. For us to have any kind of relationship with Him, we have to find a way for our sins to be forgiven. But we can do nothing to accomplish that; the debt is too big. We can't buy God's favor; we can't work for it; and we can't ever be good enough to earn it. God's holiness demanded that sin be paid for, and God's love found a way.

God loves you with an everlasting love. His love is the basis on which you can love others. All of our effort comes to nothing if you don't understand and grasp this truth: You are loved.

The greatest thing God ever did is a love story. Almighty God saw us as we really are, loved us, and said, "You guys have messed up so bad, and you're not going to be able to fix it yourself. I'm sending My own Son to provide the way back to Me." The cost was great, but the gift was extended freely because of love. Jesus humbled Himself and came into this world to be born a Baby because of love.

The greatest verse in the Bible talks about this. John 3:16 says it all: "God so loved the world, that he gave his only Son, that whoever believes in him should not perish but have eternal life."

Walk through those phrases with me:
God—the greatest lover
so loved—the greatest degree
the world—the greatest number of people
that He gave—the greatest act
His only begotten Son—the greatest gift

What evidence of this truth is revealed in the next verse, John 3:17?

Read 1 John 4:7-12, and answer the following questions.
What does loving one another prove about us?

What does not loving others prove about us?

How did God prove His love?

What is the source of our love for others?

What was God's proof of His love for us?

Why should we love others?

If no one can see God, how can the world know about His love?

Love is the greatest story ever told. Love is the greatest theme in all of Scripture. Even when He was sending His fallen ones out of the garden, God promised a way back. Then He demonstrated His love by sending His only Son into this world two thousand years ago in Bethlehem. God is love.

Those who abide in God are also love (1 John 4). When we really are connected to God in a personal way, we become loving people. As we study this concept of biblical love, we need to get specific. The idea of love in our world is so distorted it would be easy to label almost anything as love.

> What are some true or false ways you've heard love defined?
> Example: "Love is never having to say you're sorry."
> Others:

God's Word primarily describes three kinds of love. When the New Testament was written, the most commonly used word for *love* in Greek society was one of two types: a brotherly love, translated *phileo*, or a sexual love, *eros*. But the word Scripture uses most often to describe love is *agape*. This term for love was seldom used in the world at the time but was the one type of love God used most in His Word. This is the meaning of love we're going after this week.

Agape is selfless love, giving love. It can be summarized as "you before me." It describes love as an act of the will. It's a choice you make to put someone else's best interests above your own. Too often when people use the word *love*, what they're really saying is, "I feel something." Tragically, what people often mean when they say, "I love you," is not, "I've made a commitment to place your needs above my own," but instead, "I love what you do for me. You make me feel good. You are working right now for the person I love most—me." That isn't love; that's selfishness. If you build a relationship on that, you're going to have difficult days ahead.

> Review the last five or six times that you've said, "I love you," to someone.
> Were you saying, "You before me"? ☐ Yes ☐ No
> Was it motivated by your will or feelings? ☐ Yes ☐ No
> Was it, "I love what you do for me," or, "I love you; therefore, I will do this for you"?

> List some reasons you love someone special in your life.
> I love _____ because ...

> Was your first instinct to describe someone you love because it benefits you first?
> Consider what you can do to redirect your love so that it's "you before me."

Now go practice it. See you tomorrow.

God's love is not a pampering love; it's a perfecting love. God is committed to the highest good in you and me. Yesterday we focused on God's amazing love for us. Because He loves us, He wants us to grow. Part of that training will happen in our study for the rest of the week as we look at how our love can grow for the people around us.

The challenge I want to extend to you today is this: it's time to up your concept of love. As God reaches into your life through difficult circumstances, that often comes through difficult people to love, He wrenches from your grip the tools of your own tyranny, asking, "You don't really want to continue struggling with that anymore, do you? Give it to Me." God's love is for your highest good. God has dreams for you; God sees things that weigh you down, and He wants you to be released from them so that He can demonstrate His fullest work in your heart and life. That's the love He's working out. He's interested in conforming you to the image of His Son, Jesus.

With that as our goal, we turn from God's vertical love for us to our horizontal love for other people. Perhaps the best chapter in the Bible that focuses on our love for one another is 1 Corinthians 13. Open your Bible and read the 13 verses right now.

Love is the longest entry in *Webster's Dictionary of Quotable Definitions*. For 10 columns of small print, authors, poets, scholars, and preachers attempt to define *love*. Misunderstood and misused, love is often defined by what it does. The Bible has much to say about love and its transforming power in what it can do for a severed or struggling relationship or a critical attitude. Before we dive into 1 Corinthians 13, let's look at how other verses support 1 Corinthians 13 definitions.

Love is a debt worth having. "Owe no one anything, except to love each other" (Rom. 13:8).

Love keeps us thinking clearly. It clears away things that injure relationships and obscure our minds. "If we are in our right mind, it is for you. For the love of Christ controls us" (2 Cor. 5:13-14).

Love binds relationships together. "Their hearts may be encouraged, being knit together in love" (Col. 2:2).

Love keeps us fervent in our love. It moves our focus off relationship failure. "Above all, keep loving one another earnestly, since love covers a multitude of sins" (1 Pet. 4:8).

Love gives access to distant relationships. Have you tried to reach someone whose heart is hard, cold, and distant? "Through love serve one another" (Gal. 5:13).

God's love allows us to conquer every obstacle. "In all these things we are more than conquerors through him who loved us" (Rom. 8:37).

No wonder 1 Corinthians 13:13 says, "The greatest thing is love."

Go back over this list and circle a key word in each verse.

Even More Beautiful the Closer You Look

Some chapters in the Bible are well-known just by their chapter reference. First Corinthians 13 is well-known as "the love chapter." Normally your Bible doesn't turn there unless you're at a wedding. This chapter is like a beautiful flower that people admire but then file away with "white lace and promises." However, if you put 1 Corinthians 13 under a microscope and examine it closely, you'll discover that it only becomes more beautiful. The closer you look at God's definition of love, the more exquisite it becomes.

We discovered last week that we all have specific people in our lives whom we struggle to love. When we catch hold of biblical love, some phenomenal things can happen. When the people in our lives aren't living up to what they should be doing and our critical spirit kicks in, we should draw our hearts and minds back to 1 Corinthians and get to work on whatever attribute of love applies. Maybe we put on kindness or patience or give that person grace to grow in this area that is really turning your crank. Over time people will notice. You're not acting like everyone else anymore. You're different in a good way.

First Corinthians 13 gives us the nuts and bolts of loving one another; this kind of love is rooted in God's character and flows from His power at work in us. Our ability to love like God loves is the result of our abiding in Him and letting His life flow through us.

Read John 13:25.
Name some people who come to mind right now as good examples of expressing love 1 Corinthians 13-style? How do they do it?

Return to 1 Corinthians 13. Which of the descriptions of love are areas where would you like to grow?

Case Study: Conversation in the Recliner

I had just loosened my tie, kicked off my shoes, and settled back into my recliner with the sports section after a particularly rough day at work. I tried to block out the conversation happening in the kitchen between my wife and our youngest daughter, who reminded her mom that she had to be dropped at a friend's home across town. I thought: *I sure hope my wife doesn't expect me to do this. She does look swamped right now with dinner, but my work is done for the day. I wonder if my family realizes how important I am at work. People run across town, even across the country, to meet with me. Just let me close my eyes, and she'll get how tired I am and feel really guilty if she asks me to make the run. After all, I am the breadwinner in this family, and I need some time to recoup and refresh to be on top of my game. It's best for all of us. Anyway, my day has been far more taxing than my wife's. Just let her do it. I don't mind if dinner is a little late. After all, love is patient.*

In what specific ways is this man struggling with expressing biblical love?

Recall a situation in recent days where you too struggled with something similar.

Ask God to grow His agape in your life through His Spirit. As we work through verses and exercises, identify two or three aspects of love that you know you need to sharpen. Then pray to your Father, *I admire and want these qualities, but I can't produce them on my own. Lord, I'm willing to be more loving, but please do it through me.*

All God needs to begin His work is your willing spirit. Have you made yourself available to produce His fruit in your life today, this week? Keep abiding, making your home with Him, and watch Him grow His love in your life. Tell a friend about your commitment to grow more loving, and ask for your friend's support in accountability and prayer.

Case Study: Love Listens

I want to love my wife as Christ loves the church, but many times I don't know how. Even the best of intentions flop sometimes. I study her, as Pastor James encourages us husbands to be students of our wives, but different circumstances demand different responses. Does she need love that is patient, or does she need love that speaks the truth? Does she need me to love her by coming to her rescue, or am I to be her best cheerleader? I have found the only thing that works consistently is to listen to God, sincerely wanting and willing to do what is right and righteous in every situation. It always involves my attitude of "you before me." If I slow down long enough to study and talk with my wife, I can usually think and act in a way that God can use me.

Communication Without Love

"If I speak in the tongues of men and of angels, but have not love, I am a noisy gong or a clanging cymbal" (1 Cor. 13:1).

How does love enhance any and all of our communication?

Here's what happens without love. Confront without love and someone gets hurt. Correct without love and someone gets hurt. Complain without love and someone gets hurt. Condemn without love and someone gets hurt. Console without love and someone already hurt gets hurt worse. In most cases, when love is missing from the communication, everyone loses.

Read Ephesians 4:19.
Think about a recent conversation you've had with a family member, a coworker, or a friend. How could a phrase that you said have been better stated to reflect God's love?

I said:

I should have said:

Do this kind of exercise all the time, but do it quickly since we often forget the words we say and the wounds we might have inflicted. Grow in love.

Lord, thank You for 1 Corinthians 13. It's as relevant today as the day it was written. It speaks to our experience and calls us to decrease criticism and increase love—sometimes speaking truth, more often accepting and embracing people who, like me, are in the process of transformation. God, forgive my negative, critical, fault-finding ways. Give me a heart to love people and bear with them, to speak truth when it's needed, whatever the cost. I don't want merely to try harder to be more loving, Lord. Please help me love others through You. Only through my proximity to You and not through any strength of my own can I do this. Only You can give me a supernatural, endless capacity to love the people that wound or exhaust me. When I see that happening, Lord, I'll know it's You alive and working in me. In Jesus' name, amen.

How do we love? How do we take our selfish, me first attitude and turn it to "you first"? We've all tried to be loving, but sooner or later we fail miserably. The secret to living a life of love is to love in God's strength. His Spirit living in you gives you the ability to love the people in your life.

How does 2 Corinthians 5:14-15 say we can love?

How does Philippians 3:14 tell us to approach this job?

How does 1 John 4:9 say we can love others?

In the strength and love of Christ, let's dive into 1 Corinthians 13. The love chapter comes on the heels of chapter 12 that focuses on the spiritual gifts every believer has in Christ Jesus. The context flows from specific ways we serve Christ as individuals to a way we all can and must serve God as members of one another, namely by loving one another. A Christian may be able to minister in many areas, including the ability to witness, teach, or even preach; have biblical insight and knowledge, or faith, service, and giving. But these mean little without growth in the most important Christian distinctive—love.

No matter how clearly you understand God's truth or how capable you are of bringing truth to bear upon a person's life, if you don't love the people you're talking to, if you don't have a broken heart for them, you're wasting your time. How many times have we made the mistake of going to people with the truth but not having been on our knees for them?

What happens when we share God's truth with people without truly loving them?

> If a young woman entering an abortion clinic expects condemnation and you give her love, if a gay-rights activist tries to provoke you to anger and you respond in love, if an unbelieving relative attempts to destroy you and instead of retaliation you cry out in love, what will they see? They will see Jesus. He always matched His words with His actions.

This kind of love is just not possible in our own strength. Woven throughout this list is the truth that love is the fruit of God's Spirit living in us. The 15 attributes describing the qualities of love are made possible when a person's character is ruled by God. We see these character traits most clearly in the life of anyone in whose heart God's love reigns.

Love is patient. It waits. Patience extends grace, even in heated moments. Agape love, the "you before me" kind of love waits for another. It doesn't become agitated or pushy.

Make it personal. Is your anger or frustration measured in seconds, minutes, hours, or days? Patience extends grace, even in heated moments.

Love is kind. Have you ever noticed how much of Christ's life was spent in doing kind things? He spent a huge proportion of His time simply doing good. Love cares more for others than for itself. Kindness is often made obvious by what you say. Keep your words free of petty criticism and focus on words that will build others up.

Make it personal. It's easy to be kind to some people. Others are more difficult. Let someone in this second group test God's Spirit's power in you. Anyone can love a lovely person (see Luke 6:32). Are you kind to those who make you crazy? If yes, then rejoice that the Spirit is in control.

The love chapter follows these two positive expressions of love with seven expressions of what love is not..

Love is not jealous. Love doesn't want what it doesn't have. Jealousy wants to keep, and envy wants to have, but love isn't found in either. Need a key for this kind of love? Be content with what God has given you.

Make it personal. How do you handle the successes of the people you love? Love says, "I accept you even when you are more successful or more prominent than I am, even when you are more recognized and more rewarded than I am. I am for you. I have always been for you. I rejoice in your success, and I will not let a jealous outlook sour my love for you. I accept and revel in your prosperity because I love you. I won't be caught in a jealous spirit.

Love does not brag, nor is arrogant. It doesn't strut or have a swelled head. You express God's love when you adopt an accepting attitude and willingly embrace others who don't achieve all you have.

Make it personal. Romans 12:3 is a sobering check. Do you think more highly of yourself than you ought to think? Love says, "I will not make you uncomfortable by boasting in my success. I will not highlight my life in any way that embarrasses or belittles you."

Love isn't rude. It doesn't force itself on others. It doesn't develop a sharp, critical spirit, but remains tactful.

Make it personal. You act lovingly when you say the proper thing at the proper time in a loving way, regardless of what you wish you could say or you would say without the Spirit's control.

Lord, we're only halfway through the list, and I'm already overwhelmed with my lack of love. I am so convicted by this. I repent of my selfish, me-first attitudes and turn to You in repentance and faith. Only You can change me. Thank You for putting the desire in my heart to see Your Spirit's fruit grow in me. Increase my love for Your children. Increase my patience, my kindness, my humility so that Your character is seen in me. Thank You in advance for working in my heart. Please don't stop. In Your great love, amen.

My God and my love, You are mine and I am Yours. Deepen Your love in me, O Lord, that I may learn how joyful it is to serve You. Let Your love take hold of me and raise me above myself, that I may be filled with devotion because of Your goodness. Then I will sing a song to You of love. I will follow You, and my soul will never grow tired of praising You. Let me love You more than myself and love myself only for Your sake. Let me love all others in You and for You, as Your law of love commands. Amen
—Thomas a' Kempis

Love is the bumper sticker of our faith. If we need a fish on our car to convince the world that we love Jesus, then we know little of Him. He said we should display our discipleship to Him by loving one another (John 13:35). Love is our bumper sticker.

Of all the things it could be, why did Jesus say love? Maybe because Satan has no counterfeit for it. It's the most unexpected act we can do. In a self-seeking, get-out-of-my way world, an unselfish act of pure love is the strike of a match in pitch blackness. It's so different and so welcome that all who see it take notice. The world is all too familiar with a selfish, hateful response. It never expects love.

We're continuing our study of agape love. We've looked at these aspects: Love is patient. Love is kind. Love is not jealous. Love does not brag. Love isn't arrogant. Love is not rude. Return to 1 Corinthians 13 and pick up our study at verse 5:

Love is not selfish. Love doesn't have to be first. Love doesn't insist on its own way. Unselfish people can't say, "I did it my way." They say, "You before me."

Make it personal. In what way are you saying, "Me before you?" In what areas can you bend to someone else's way?

Love is not short-tempered. Love doesn't fly off the handle. Love values the person behind the frustration.

Make it personal. Are you quickest to bark at the ones you say you love most, saving your most polite behavior for business associates, church members, or even strangers? How can you apply this aspect of love to those you love?

Love doesn't keep accounts of wrongs suffered. Love doesn't keep score. Want to show God's love? Forget about the grudge you've been carrying.

Make it personal. Which characterizes you best: I turn the other cheek, or I'm all about seeking revenge? Are you able to forgive and forget, or do you need a computer to keep score of all the perceived wrongs against you? How does this aspect of love apply to you?

Love finds no pleasure in wrongdoing. Love doesn't play games. Love says, "You're important to God and to me." Let that attitude direct your actions and interactions.

Make it personal. How long do you let people feel their sin? Love lets the repentant heart off the hook. Do you need to ask someone for forgiveness? Do you need to forgive someone?

Although an act of love can be as quiet as a whisper—even anonymous—the act itself screams of God. This is God's loudspeaker of truth to the world, and we are to display it visibly wherever we go. "Let us not love with words or tongue but with actions and in truth" (1 John 3:18, NIV)

Love never fails. Think about the implications of the promise that God is making there. Love will never fail to accomplish God's highest and best purposes. Love improves every situation. If you pursue it with your whole heart and embrace the people in your life as they are, even when they hurt you, God will use that. Love will never fail you at work. It won't fail you at home. It won't fail you in the church. What a promise! Love never fails.

Make it personal. Have you given up on some people in your life? Is a relationship so damaged that it cannot be restored? How does this compare with God's love? Pray today for people like this in your life.

Love rejoices with the truth. Love and truth are partners. You can't have love without truth or truth without love. When you love others, you edify them with freedom to speak the truth.

Make it personal. Have you avoided speaking the truth in love? Is there someone in your life right now for whom you are concerned, with whom you should speak the truth in love? Pray about and plan what you can say, making sure you balance truth and love.

Love bears with someone. Love puts up with the peculiarities of others. Love bears the weight of misunderstanding. To bear with someone means to cover over, so as to protect or to shield. When others disappoint you, love keeps you from getting sidetracked.

Make it personal. Do you need to show love right now by protecting or shielding someone?

Love believes all things. Love trusts God. Love has an incurable confidence that God is at work in other people's lives and never gives up looking out for their best. Love defends another. Love finds itself saying on a regular basis, "That's not what she meant. That's not why he did that." Love doesn't judge motives. We don't know why people do what they do, but love always believes the best.

Make it personal. Do you trust yourself and your own judgment more than God's? Are you more likely to express judgment/criticism or love? Do you tend to believe the best or the worst about others? If loving trust is difficult for you, pray for God to change your heart right now.
Lord, is this Your word for me?

Love hopes all things. Looks for the best. When you give others the benefit of the doubt, you show them God's love.

Make it personal. Do you see people not as they are but as they will be by God's grace? To whom does this apply in your life?

Love endures all things. Love has faith to see the end. Love remains under the weight until the season has taken its course. Love stays put. Endure is a military term meaning "to drive a stake in the ground." Love says: "I'm going to love you. You can retreat if you want, but I'm never going back from this place right here. I'm going to be there for you."

Make it personal. Can people in your life depend on your enduring love, or is your love conditional on their behavior as it meets your needs? Express to those you love that because of God's love in you, your love for them will endure, regardless of what they do or don't do.

The power of the love that endures all things and makes commitments to one another is what biblical commitment is all about. I've loved this last word on a love that endures: "Brother, I want you to know that I'm committed to you. You will never knowingly suffer at my hands. I will never say anything or do anything knowingly to hurt you. I will always, in every circumstance, seek to help and support you. If you're down and I can lift you up, I'll do that. If you need something and I have it, I'll share it with you. If you need it, I'll give it to you. No matter what I find out about you, no matter what happens in the future—good or bad—my commitment to you will never change. And there is nothing you can do about it. You don't have to respond. I love you." And that's what enduring love is.

Match love's description with its definition.

_____ 1. Love is patient.	a. It doesn't want what it doesn't have.
_____ 2. Love is kind.	b. It lasts.
_____ 3. Love does not envy.	c. It looks for the best.
_____ 4. Love does not boast.	d. It does not act unbecomingly.
_____ 5. Love is not arrogant.	e. It doesn't think too highly of itself.
_____ 6. Love is not rude.	f. It waits.
_____ 7. Love does not insist on its own way.	g. It isn't selfish.
_____ 8. Love is not irritable.	h. It does not brag.
_____ 9. Love is not resentful.	i. It isn't short-tempered.
_____ 10. Love does not rejoice at wrongdoing.	j. It doesn't revel when others suffer.
_____ 11. Love rejoices with the truth.	k. It practices good for another's benefit.
_____ 12. Love bears all things.	l. It edifies when it says it like it is.
_____ 13. Love believes all things.	m. It perseveres.
_____ 14. Love hopes all things.	n. It still has faith in another.
_____ 15. Love endures all things.	o. It trusts God always.
_____ 16. Love never ends.	p. It forgives.

Answers. 1-F, 2-K, 3-A, 4-H, 5-E, 6-D, 7-G, 8-I, 9-P, 10-J, 11-L, 12-M, 13-O, 14-C, 15-N, 16-B

Choose five definitions/descriptions of love from the list above and describe how each can show up in your life when God is in control. Give specifics.

Example: Love is patient. When God is in control, I can be patient when my husband comes home late from work. I sincerely try to understand when he says it is beyond his control. I appreciate his valuing family time as much as he does his job and trust him to come home as soon as his job allows.

1. Love is/does

When God is in control, I can be

2. Love is/does

When God is in control, I can be

3. Love is/does

When God is in control, I can be

4. Love is/does

When God is in control, I can be

5. Love is/does

When God is in control, I can be

What Is Their Love Language?

Gary Chapman wrote a wise book about horizontal love called *The Five Love Languages*. Its premise is that people communicate and receive love in different ways. If you care about how effectively you communicate your love, you'll pick up this tool as soon as possible.

Here it is in a nutshell. People feel loved in five dominant ways. Your specific combination is your love language. Maybe you don't care as much about receiving thoughtful gifts from your family, friends, or spouse; but you would give anything for a heart-to-heart conversation with them. Perhaps your love language is someone helping you with something you need like taking out the trash, building a patio, or putting gas in your car. These describe scenarios; now examine the categories of love languages:

Words of Affirmation. Spoken words, written words, whispered words. Kind words received feel like a pat on the back or a warm hug. Words of affirmation come in through the ears and go directly to your heart.

Quality Time. I want an evening of you. Turn off your phone, the stereo, and the TV. I want focused, quality time.

Receiving Gifts. If your love language is receiving gifts, your birthday and Christmas are a big deal, especially if the gift was thoughtful or personal. Other people don't get the connection between gifts and love; they'd rather you'd give them (time alone with them/a hug/help/a phone call).

Acts of Service or Deeds of Kindness. Someone who speaks this language feels loved when you serve them in small or large ways.

Physical Touch. Ever notice how some people are huggers while others are not? This group loves to touch, hold hands, and sit close.

> Identify the love language of your family members and close friends. How do they feel loved?
>
> Name   Love Language
>
> Name   Love Language
>
> Name   Love Language
>
> Name   Love Language
>
> Name   Love Language

The way you naturally express love is most likely your love language. Consider this. Are you loving the people in your life according to their love language or your own?

Father, thank You for the work that You have been doing and will do in every yielded, responsive heart. We ask that You continue to be with us as we move through these pages. Give us teachable hearts, O God. The days are short, but the opportunities are great to experience Your love and to live according to Your Word as we love others. Cause each of us to be loving, as You have been and are our example. We ask in Jesus' name, amen.

If you're growing in your faith and in your walk with the Lord, you're becoming a more loving person; but none of that happens in a vacuum. In community many opportunities challenge love.

One issue we've not yet discussed is the balance between love and truth. All love and no truth is hypocrisy. All truth and no love is brutality. So how do you know what to do? Here are some guidelines. See the issues in your relationships as major and minor. On the majors don't play games. In every relationship some issues are serious. What are those issues?

Is this path critical?	Failure to take action will produce major fallout.	Ex: Major doctrinal error, marital unfaithfulness, criminal acts, abusive behavior
Is the problem chronic?	You see the same thing happening over and over.	Ex: Addictive behaviors, character flaws, blind spots
Does your proximity imply responsibility?	Things we can live with	Ex: Excessive spending in our neighbors and friends but we can't live with in our spouse and kids.

In these cases, love does not sit passively by and say, "I love him so I won't upset him." Wrong! Love takes action on things that are major.

> Considering the list of love's characteristics we've been studying this week, describe how those confrontations on major issues should be carried out:

Nobody should pretend to have all the answers. However, sometimes a serious word and follow-through are needed for a major issue. And sometimes, sadly, people walk away. But those who bear up under the weight of the truth, remain under the pressure, and love one another through tough times of truth experience phenomenal growth.

Minor issues offer opportunities for acceptance. If you were to list a hundred things that could possibly require confronting your boss, your spouse, or your neighbor, maybe three items on that list could fit in the category we just called major. The other 97 are minor. They only irritate you because of your own sinfulness and pride. We are prone to take minor molehills and make them into major mountains, and in that soil a critical spirit can flourish and grow.

Minors are matters of personal preference. What are some examples of minors that test your ability to love others?

Ex: their choice of music

Caught in Conversation

"It recently dawned on me that if love is the greatest command, then unloving, selfish, or hateful acts would be among the greatest of sins. Unfortunately, these acts are also among the most common." ☐ **Agree** ☐ **Disagree** Why?

"Because of this realization, I began to pray a simple prayer: 'Jesus, teach me how to love.' As a result, He is sensitizing me to my unloving actions such as impatience, a sharp tongue, and a judging heart, while reminding me how the testimony of Jesus in my life depends on my ability to love. Without love I'm a fake." ☐ **Agree** ☐ **Disagree**
How does love speak to a consistent Christian life?

Before your feet hit the floor in the morning, ask, "Lord, teach me to love today."

What habit, as described above, would you like God to change in you to reflect what you believe? Three are listed, fill in your personal list:
impatience
a sharp tongue
a judging heart

What opportunities do you see to apply this in everyday life? Make a statement like this:
I determine, in God's strength, to be more patient with fast-food clerks, store salespeople, and phone operators. I will not be a fake about my faith.

Now write your own.
I determine, in God's strength

Case Study: Balancing Love and Truth

My friend has a drinking problem. I can tell it by his breath. I can see it in his eyes. I know it by his actions. I know that he is hurting himself and his family. So what do I do?

Truth Without Grace. Man, you've been drinking again, haven't you? Don't deny it. It's obvious. Don't you know you're on a path of self-destruction? Do you realize how much you're hurting yourself, your family, and your friends? Don't you know you're hurting the name of the Lord Jesus Christ? Is that what you want? You really need to take a hard look at yourself and where this path is taking you and once and for all give up that godless, filthy habit.

Grace Without Truth. Brother, I know you're hurting. I know life isn't going the way you'd like it to go. If I can do anything for you, all you need to do is let me know. I'll give you a ride anywhere you need to go. If you lose your job, you can live with us. When others condemn you, I'll take your side.

It's not about balancing truth and love; we need a paradigm shift. We are not supposed to be balancing love and truth as though they are separate things. According to 1 Corinthians 13, truth is part of love, and you're not really loving if speaking truth is not part of that relationship. All truth and no love is brutality. But all love and no truth is just playing games with people. Without truth any expression of love is crippled. Love can only be fired up about what is true and what is right.

Now it's your turn. How would you respond, balancing love and truth?

How much energy does God have regarding our love for one another? Read the following verses and choose a few to memorize and incorporate in your daily living.

John 15:12	Galatians 5:14	Ephesians 5:2
Romans 12:10	Hebrews 10:24	1 Peter 4:8
1 Corinthians 16:14	1 John 3:11	1 John 4:21

Case Study: Small-Group Love

Our small group, eight people—three couples and two singles—realized that we weren't making progress in doing life together. We met faithfully, but when our meeting was over each Wednesday night, we hardly thought of one another until the next week. That all changed when we determined we were going to work at loving one another. We made this vow and are really growing in our faith and in amazing relationship. We vowed to:

1. Lose ourselves in others. It's about you, not me.
2. Listen deeply and hear what someone is saying and not saying.
3. Love the unlovely in our group and in our community.
4. Leave our mistakes at the foot of the cross and forgive one another.
5. Discover God's plan for our lives. We pray and seek the Lord for one another.
6. Lean on the power of the Holy Spirit when we don't know how to help or pray for one another.
7. Lead others to Christ.

Does your small group need some new commitments? Love is the badge and character of Christianity. If you are growing in your love for others, then you are growing as a Christian.

Loving Father, we love because You loved us first. We know love because we know You. Thank You for the countless ways You are growing and teaching us to be more like Your Son as we model His life of love. In the areas in which we're still growing, thank You for bearing with us. Enable us by Your Spirit's power to love others with Your agape love. Bring these teachings from Your Word to bear upon our lives. Let others notice the difference and remark, "See how they love one another." We want to be known as Your disciples so please, Lord, continue to teach us how to love as You love. In Your great love we pray, amen.

"Be imitators of God, as beloved children. And walk in love, as Christ loved us and gave himself up for us, a fragrant offering and sacrifice to God."
Ephesians 5:1-2

REPLACE A DOUBTING ATTITUDE ...

In small groups begin by telling about someone you love and why you love him or her. Then share situations from the past week when you've tried to implement agape you-before-me love.

1. Where do we get the power to love people the way God wants us to love them?

2. Why is love considered to be "the greatest of these"?

3. In what ways is love most often self-centered?

4. What does agape love look like?

5. What do you do when an issue barges into your relationship?

Psalm 84 : 11
Promise of
Deut. 1 : 20-21 ; 28-30 ; 31

Hebrew 11:6
Numbers 13: 2-3 ; 17-20 ; 25-26, 27-29 ; 30 ; 31
Phillippians 4:19 Promise of Provision
Isaiah 54:17 Promise of protection

Discussion Questions
About Love

Video

Back in the desert again, we are going to deal with a doubting attitude. Watch and listen for what the Scripture says and to learn whether you have a doubting attitude.

Will you trust God or won't you?
Faith is an attitude

Video Notes

Doubt is the __absence__ of faith.

Doubt is a lack of confidence or assurance that God will keep His __promises__.

God places regular tests of __faith__ in front of His children.

Faith is not a part of the Christian life; it's the __whole__ thing.

Are you going to pass the test of faith?

The circumstances of life will shrink or __stretch__ your faith.

Doubt sees the obstacles; faith sees the __opportunities__.

Faith is not part of the Christian life; it is th[e] whole thing

Heb. 11:6 Eph 2:8 Col 2:6

Obstacles to Faith

1. Fear
2. Anger
3. Withdrawal
4. Bitterness
5. The Facts

When surrounded by doubters, doubting comes easily. Num. 14:1-2

Doubt is contagious.

Doubt is passive. (do nothing)
Doubting starts
Doubters are easier to find than friends of faith.

It's a short journey from doubt to despair.

Numbers 14:3-4

Despair plans come from despairing hearts

1. Can faith and doubt coexist?

2. How do the obstacles to faith lead to doubt?

3. How does doubt affect your relationship with God?

4. How does doubt affect your Christian witness?

5. What verse of Scripture strengthens you when doubts arise?

Discussion Questions
About a Doubting Attitude

Study **Challenge**

Do you have a doubting attitude? Take a close look this week to uncover your doubts. Let the Scriptures speak to you as you ask God to help you change your attitude.

Memory Verse

"But let him ask in faith, with no doubting, for the one who doubts is like a wave of the sea that is driven and tossed by the wind."
James 1:6

Christians don't generally set out to doubt God. They don't bring their faith into question without reason. For most of us, life's pain simply catches us off guard. The reality of hardship trips us up.

Doubt, taken directly to the Lord, leads to faith because God's Word and God's character can stand under the most microscopic scrutiny. But left on your own in your grief or difficult circumstances, left to entertain your own questions, alone to stir your circular reasoning, or even worse, left alone in the company of other doubters or bitter people, doubt can grow rapidly.

First, let's define *doubt*. Doubt is an unsettled opinion about the certainty of something. Doubt is not unbelief. Unbelief is different and more dangerous. Unbelief is refusal to believe something regardless of any evidence. Doubt is just unsettledness. Unbelief is a refusal to believe. However, doubt, if left alone too long, can lead to unbelief. Doubt is a lack of confidence or assurance that God will keep His promises.

What you believe about God is the most important thing about you. It shapes your life and determines how you deal with good and hard things that come your way. It has everything to do with how your life will be lived and how much victory or defeat you will know. If that is true, then how God feels about your doubt is extremely significant.

> Consider these metaphors and similes for doubt:
> Doubt is cancer of the soul.
> Doubt is like a machete to your garden.
> Doubt is like a match to your house.
> Doubt is the toxin that eats away at the fabric of your relationship with God.
>
> Now come up with your own word picture of doubt.

> Can you think of a time in your life when you doubted that God would keep His promises? What happened? What turned your mind and heart around?

Faith is something we grow into; doubt is something we grow out of.

Or perhaps doubt sometimes still nips at your heels. Don't let doubt turn to despair. Watch for help in this week's study and next week's study on replacing a doubting attitude with faith.

Where Does Doubt Come From?

Doubt comes in many forms and ways. Doubt may be triggered by hardship and suffering or by the effort to make faith fit with the painful realities of life: Someone you love dies. Innocent people suffer. You lose a marriage, a job, or your health. Faith is put to the test, and you question your faith. You scramble to hold back your doubts. Doubt can come from pain.

Doubt is a lack of confidence or assurance that God will keep His promises.

Doubt can come from spending more time looking at the newspaper than looking to God. Doubters might say, "The world is so messed up. I can't reconcile a God of love with a world so filled with suffering! If God is real, how do you explain natural disasters, wars, and poverty?" A lot of people feel this way because they cannot put God and what they see together.

Doubt may also come from legitimate questions. Perceived contradictions in the Bible, miracles like the virgin birth, incongruities in Gospel accounts, and phenomenal acts like creation can evoke questions. Doubt surfaces when faith is required for belief. I call this the "Disillusioned Doubter." Believing requires conclusions doubters don't see.

Doubt also springs from unbelief. Doubt and unbelief are not the same. Sometimes doubt is faith staggering for firm footing. Sometimes, though, doubt becomes a rebellion against faith itself. Then it's disbelief.

> Label the following verses and statements "Doubt" or "Disbelief."
> Mark 9:24   Hebrews 4:2
> "I can't ..."   "I won't ..."

This is the kind of doubt the children of Israel nurtured in the desert. They used the doubt born out of the upheaval in their lives to rationalize disobedience. Honest doubt ("How will the Lord take care of us out here?") became simply embellished sin ("I don't believe He will"). They turned a difficult circumstance into a wilderness by the choice not to believe God would do what He promised.

When the author of Hebrews in the New Testament was urging his audience to keep going on in their faith in spite of the hardship faced, he cautioned that "no one ... fall by following [Israel's] example of disobedience" (Heb 4:11, NIV).

> When doubt takes hold of us, what does Hebrews 4:11-12 remind us to do?

> In what ways have you been tempted or seen others tempted to use doubt as an excuse to resist what God is asking of you? For example, has He ever asked you to trust Him in something hard and doubt made you drag your feet?

> How has Scripture helped you obey?

Doubt erupts from our pain. The choice that determines whether you will live in the wilderness or be on your way to the land God promises is this: Will you bring your questions to God who hurts along with you, even if you must wait for satisfying answers?

In this lesson we're going back to the wilderness with the children of Israel to retrace their path. Our goal is to learn from them, as Hebrews 4 tells us to, and not to follow in their footsteps.

When we struggle with doubting God, we need to ask ourselves: What do we know about His character? How does He work? What has been our source of revelation? His Word? other people? How does all of this relate to the current situation?

The children of Israel had no reason to doubt God's promises. Every time He said He would do something, He did it. Think about their recent history.

At the beginning of the Exodus, God proved Himself to His people in Egypt, performing incredible signs and wonders, including His judgment on Egypt on 10 separate occasions. Through it all He had kept the Israelites safe (see, for example, Ex. 9:26; 14:29). Yet days after their miraculous escape at the Red Sea, they didn't seem to have a shred of faith in God's ability to save them (see Ex. 14:12).

During the trek to the promised land, God supernaturally provided for every need the people faced. There were no grocery stores, yet Israel would be fed with manna from heaven. There was no water, but the Lord would bring forth springs from a rock to quench their thirst. There were no stores, but the people's clothes and shoes never wore out.

God gave them a physical sign of His presence and directions—a cloud by day that also protected them from the blazing desert sun and at night a supernatural fire that warmed them from the desert chill. Yet Israel responded with infrequent responses of faith that caved in when they faced the next challenge.

At the entrance to the promised land, God promised victory in Canaan, but the people refused to believe God was bigger than "the giants in the land." Finally God said, "Enough." Israel had slapped away God's good hand too many times, and now all of them except Caleb and Joshua would spend the rest of their lives in the wilderness.

> Write here your thoughts regarding Israel's fear, bitterness, anxiety, and their lack of confidence that God would keep His promises. How does this account of the way God's people acted make you feel? Realistically, what should have been their response to God?

Let's draw some principles from their wilderness mistakes to apply in our own lives today.

God places regular tests in front of us. With our response either we get closer to Him and more filled with faith, or we get farther away from Him and more filled with doubt.

Lesson 1 from the Wilderness of Doubt
The circumstances of life will either shrink or stretch your faith.

As the entire crowd of Israelites camped at the border of the promised land, Moses chose and sent out 12 men who would check out what the land was like and whether the people who lived in it were strong or weak. Is the land fat or lean? Trees or no trees? And he said, "Be of good courage and bring some of the fruit of the land" (Ex. 13:20). (They were hungry for something other than manna, you know.)

Read Numbers 13:4-24.

The spies went up into the land. What did they see?

What was their report? Would they take the land God told them He would provide?

Read Deuteronomy 1:19-33.

What had God told them before they entered the land?

How did Moses describe God's care for them through the desert?

According to verses 20-21, what was God's original plan for entering the land?

How did Moses characterize the people's response to the scouts (vv. 26,32)?

Why do you think God tested these people? Why not just bring them into the land by some miracle?

Read Numbers 13:25-33.

What was the difference in response between Caleb and Joshua, the spies whose faith was stretched, and the other 10 whose faith was shrunk by their circumstances?

What words in the spies' reports reveal their attitude of doubt or faith regarding the circumstances?

The spies were great examples for us of doubt and faith. The situation may have seemed overwhelming, but either they were going to choose to trust God or shrink in doubt.

Is anything going on in your life that's shrinking or stretching your faith? Describe it here:

God places regular tests of faith in front of us. In response we choose to get closer to Him and more filled with faith, or we get farther away from Him and more filled with doubt.

Lesson 2 from the Wilderness of Doubt
Doubting comes easily when you're surrounded by doubters.

The spies were in the land for 40 days, and the people waited to hear their report. What a night of victory this could have been! When the spies got back, they should have been whooping it up. "The land is all that God has promised us! We're taking the land! Sure, the armies are big and the people are big, but our God is bigger! He has never let us down before! Do you remember the plagues? Do you remember the Red Sea? Do you remember Mount Sinai?" They should have been going crazy with confidence in God because of all they had seen Him do for them. But they weren't. In spite of His protection in the past, to whom were the people listening? The doubters.

Read Numbers 14:1.

What were the people saying?

When surrounded by doubters, doubting comes easily. Do you have doubters in your life? How can you guard your heart from their influence?

Lesson 3 from the Wilderness of Doubt
It's a short journey from doubt to despair.

Read Numbers 14:2-3.

What did they doubt God would do?

How does this compare to what we learned about God's care in Deuteronomy 1:31?

What desperate plan did the people put together in their despair (Num. 14:4)?

Why was this plan such a bad idea? What were they forgetting about how they got there in the first place?

Why was this attitude such an insult to God?

Israel faced no danger whatsoever because God provided for them at every turn. Yet He couldn't provide trust and faith. Even after God's many miraculous provisions for Israel, His people continued to doubt Him.

Consider this: Has there been a situation in your life lately in which you've doubted what God has promised to do? Pause here and ask the Lord to reveal to you an area where you need to trust Him.

WEEK 7. DAY 3. I DOUBT IT

You can't do a Bible study on the issue of doubt without an introduction to the man who's famous for it.

Fill in the blank. Doubting _____.

If you said Thomas, you're right. Jesus recruited Thomas along with the other disciples. Those 12 men had followed Jesus for three years. We meet Thomas three times in the Gospel of John.

The first time, in John 11, Jesus was telling the disciples that He was going to Jerusalem and would suffer many things. None of the disciples really wanted to say anything, but notice what Thomas says in John 11:16, NKJV: "Then Thomas … said to his fellow disciples, 'Let us also go, that we may die with Him.'"

What does this imply about Thomas' commitment level?

Wherever Jesus went, Thomas wanted to go, even if it meant he'd have to die with Him. He was not some wavering weakling. This guy really wanted to believe.

In John 14 we meet Thomas again. Jesus was preparing His disciples for His departure. He said in verses 3-4, "And if I go and prepare a place for you, I will come again and will take you to myself, that where I am you may be also. And you know the way to where I am going."

Who piped up? .

What was his question?

How did Jesus respond (v. 6)?

Jesus was talking to Thomas. Thomas was a disciple who hadn't stopped thinking. He had the courage to question, to raise his hand and say to the Teacher, "Wait. I don't understand. That's not clear to me."

What kind of doubter was Thomas? Was Thomas …
_____ a discouraged doubter?
_____ an intellectual doubter?
_____ given to disbelief?

The last time we meet Thomas is his signature moment.

Read John 19:16-30. Do you think Thomas, as well as the other disciples (minus John) watched this scene from a distance? What must they have been thinking and feeling?

Fast-forward to John 20 and read verses 19-29.
Summarize what happened.

What day of the week was it?

What normally happens on this day?

Where was Thomas?

Instead of being with the other disciples and worshiping God, as is the believer's practice, Thomas was withdrawing. He was pulling back from others and putting up a wall. He was not willing to draw close to the Lord. Obviously he was struggling. The events of the last few days had left their marks. He was aching over Jesus' death, but he didn't get together with the others. He had isolated himself, struggling all by himself. That is a dangerous decision, then and now.

What happens when you stew about something all by yourself?
☐ The doubts go away.　　☐ The doubts get bigger.

How does your mind work? What happens if you're worried or doubtful or negative and you keep it to yourself too long? How important is a godly friend in those times?

With hopes dashed and dreams lost, Thomas was somewhere on the street or the hillside—grieving, struggling, doubting. He might have spent the night out under the stars. All the while, Jesus came back and presented Himself to the 10. The next time Thomas got with the team, they wouldn't stop talking about what had happened.

Thomas was coming back from his nighttime grief and overwhelming feelings of doubt. He said, "Sorry, guys, I'm just not there yet." Then, "Unless I see in his hands the mark of the nails, and place my finger into the mark of the nails, and place my hand into his side, I will never believe'" (v. 25).

All Thomas wanted was to see what the other guys had seen. I think he was sincere. I think he really wanted to believe. Then eight days later Jesus appeared right in the middle of the disciples, this time including Thomas.

What do you think is significant about Jesus' appearing again to the disciples eight days later?

What do you think Thomas was thinking about during this week?

With the word *peace*, Jesus reentered the scene (John 20:26-28). His attention was on Thomas. Obviously He knew of Thomas's struggle so He said, "Put your finger here, and see my hands; and put out your hand, and place it in my side. Do not disbelieve, but believe" (v. 27).

His words to Thomas were not condemning. Jesus did not rebuke Thomas for not believing the unbelievable truth that He is alive again. The one who was so insistent on proof a week ago broke down. He didn't want to put his finger in the nail prints or thrust his hand into Jesus' side. He became a believer in the truest sense of the word. He gasped, "My Lord and my God!" (v. 28).

There was no halfway with Thomas. He had fought his way through the minefield of doubt, and suddenly he was standing in front of a miracle. He surrendered, "My Lord and my God!"

Do you think it's right or wrong to struggle to believe or to want proof? To what extent?

Jesus said, "Thomas, because you have seen Me, you have believed." Then He put this part in for me and you. "Blessed are those who have not seen and yet have believed" (v. 29, NKJV). Blessed are you reading this now if you believe, having never seen Jesus' hands. Blessed are those who find in Christ the source of their faith to overcome their doubts.

Suppose Thomas was in your small group. How would he have described this event in his own words? What challenge would he offer someone who has his same tendencies?

God will go a long way in revealing Himself to a person who really wants to believe.

How Other People in the Bible Dealt with Doubt
God understands doubt; He understands the questions that would drive us to plead with Him to change life's agenda. But He gives us the example of His choice servants who experienced doubt and let it stretch their faith in God. How did these saints deal with doubt?

1. Read Job 19:25-26. How did Job bolster his faith by remembering God?

2. Read Lamentations 3:22-24. When his worst fears for his nation came true, what did Jeremiah remember about God?

3. Read Psalm 42:9-11. When David struggled with doubt, where did he direct his thinking?

4. Read Mark 9:17-24. What does this desperate father plead with Jesus to give him (v. 24)? Can you identify with his request? How?

5. Read 2 Corinthians 4:8-12. What was Paul's perspective on the suffering believers face? What purpose do suffering and faith serve?

Case Study: I Don't Believe Anymore

"I don't know what I believe anymore. I don't even know if I'm a Christian." My husband Tom's admission of his doubt shook me to the core, and his honest statement threw aftershocks into our family. Two years before, my husband's parents, a great Christian couple divorced after 30 years of marriage. Soon after that Tom's brother was diagnosed with aggressive cancer. Now we spend every weekend driving to his brother and wife's home two hours away to do small jobs around their house or visit him in hospice care. The end of my brother-in-law's life seems near. Now, out of the blue, Tom made this earth-shattering statement. "How could God allow all this suffering? I can't put it all together. The God I committed my life to seems to have tricked me into trusting Him."

Now, months later, we've done all the talking, all the arguing, all the crying we're going to do. I'm done leaving apologetic books around the house and my Bible open to the underlined passages that I remember were Tom's favorites. I'm saddened to sit in church alone. I miss praying with Tom. This isn't going to be a short, praise-the-Lord turn-around. What do I do now?

1. Have you ever known anyone who struggled like Tom or his wife? ☐ Yes ☐ No

2. What does Tom need to redirect his thinking back to the Lord?

3. What encouragement does his wife need to persevere with Tom? to persevere in her own faith?

How to Help a Doubting Friend

Consider this scenario: In the past I went to her with my questions and my struggles of faith. Now, years later, my girlfriend from church is struggling herself. She doesn't let everyone know, but I can see it in her eyes, and I notice her lack of passion during worship. She's just not herself. Her life has been overshadowed by some devastating circumstances lately; and she's trying, unsuccessfully sometimes, to make her life and faith agree. I want to help her as she has helped me. What should I do?

Listen. Pretty simple, right? Listening can be the first step to helping your friend work out her doubt. Job isn't the only one who has been deeply hurt by people who spoke when they should have listened and judged when they should have let God read his friend's thoughts and motives. Many struggles related to hardship gradually get resolved by simply talking and listening. Let her talk. You listen.

Try to determine the source of her doubt. If it is some painful experience, don't rush ahead with answers. Grief takes time. If the questions are honest and sincere, suggest a way she can get answers—through someone in your church, helpful books, or ministry Web sites that focus on intellectual reasoning. Don't argue (2 Tim. 2:23-24), and don't be afraid to admit you don't have all the answers. If the source of doubt is disbelief, carefully warn her of the consequences. Plead with her to see her circumstance through eyes of faith. .

Ask key questions. But ask in a way that doesn't sound like you're preaching. Be interested in getting to the real issue.

Use Scripture wisely. Don't be patronizing in quoting verses she already knows. Be careful of your tone of voice. Let Scripture do its work. We can say all the wise things in the world, but Scripture has the power to change someone's heart.

> What challenging words has the Lord used in your life to draw you from doubt to faith?
> Did they come through His Word? His people? from something you read?

> If you were to help someone today who is struggling with doubt, how could you use your own spiritual journey to remind them of God's character?

Lord, sometimes my fears overwhelm what I believe. I sometimes doubt whether You will fulfill the promises in Your Word to care for me. Thank You for accepting me in my struggles and understanding my questions. Thank You for knowing that when I cry or struggle I still love You. When I question the tragedies and calamities of life, it isn't that I doubt Your right to work and to rule; it's that I struggle with releasing my own rights and my own desire to reason my own way through this valley. Thank You for Your Book, which includes people like Thomas, who finally said, "My Lord and my God!" Help me come to the same conclusion—more quickly, like the centurion. I do believe You; help me when I doubt! In Your strength I will choose faith as my first response rather than listen to my fears. Thank You for drawing me to You in increased faith. May Your life be seen in me, controlling me more and more as I surrender myself to You. Do it Your way, Lord. Just help me in the process. Amen.

Christians are sometimes genuinely puzzled, asking, "Why is trusting God so hard? God has been faithful to me. God has provided for me. He's done a lot of good things in my life. Why does doubt come so easily?" Here are some reasons I've observed that come from wilderness attitudes:

Doubting is contagious. It's easier to catch than the common cold. You're kidding yourself if you think you'll come out OK when surrounded by people whose lives are filled with doubt.

> What were the people doubting in Exodus 32:1?

> What in Numbers 11:10 gives us a clue that the Israelites were passing doubt around?

Doubting is passive. Faith requires action; doubting does not. Nobody ever wakes up in the morning and says, "I bet today's going to be a great day for doubting. I'm going to doubt God all day today." Doubting is what takes over when you do nothing.

Instead of talking often about God's grace and recalling His miracles and thinking about all that He has done, people choose to focus on the obstacles; they welcome doubt. Once you get that wave going in a group, everybody rides it.

Doubting satisfies our tendency toward self-protection. Nobody likes to be wrong. "What if I step out in faith and trust God for great things, and then nothing happens? I'm going to look really dumb. It's just easier not to trust God. I'll lower my expectations so I won't be disappointed." But you are disappointed because of your doubt.

> How do the people's doubts in Numbers 14:3 negate how far they've come? Why did they want this?

Doubters are easier to find than friends of faith. How many real friends of faith do you have? Who speaks the Word of God into your life and fires you up spiritually? It's absolutely critical that we cherish those people in our lives and develop those relationships. Why? Because faith grows in the context of fellowship with other believers. Faith does not grow in isolation.

Are you treating the Christian life as something private? Are you connected to other believers? Has anyone asked you a pointed question about your spiritual life recently? If you're doing your own thing, your faith is suffering because of it. Faith grows in connectedness with other believers and in His church. God gives us friends of faith to stir us on. Don't live the Christian life alone.

> Record some specific instances of how God has worked in your life. Return to this page, add to it, or reread it as a reminder in times when doubt creeps in.

> 1. How did you see God's hand at work leading to your salvation? How did you meet the people who led you to Christ?

2. What kinds of sin in your life did God forgive and forget?

3. List ways you have seen God provide in a noteworthy way—a job, a spouse, money for a special need, and so forth.

4. List some everyday riches, gifts from God that you may take for granted: people who love you, a Bible and spiritual resources, shelter, food, clothing, and so forth.

5. Think back to when you first became a Christian. How have you changed? What are some areas of your life that God has transformed or is transforming?

6. Recall times in your life when you struggled with doubt. How do you see now that this attitude led you into a spiritual wilderness?

7. Are you out of the wilderness of doubt? What attitude helped you out, or what keeps you there?

What Is Your Testimony?

Tell someone this week about a time when you trusted God and He was faithful to His Word.

In the space below write about a time when you experienced His faithfulness, His goodness, His power to do anything.

How has the Lord recently reaffirmed His trustworthy character to you?

I have never in my life trusted God and regretted it. But I could fill pages with stories from the times in my life when I've failed to trust God and made bad choices because I wouldn't trust Him. God has never let me down! You don't have to be worried about whether you can trust God. God will be faithful to Himself and to His Word.

What if you couldn't think of anything to write? How can you get rid of all your doubts about God? Those are honest questions that have answers.

Questions to Ask if You Are Doubting

1. Have I had consistent time in God's Word on my own?
2. Have I given time and attention to conversations with the Lord? Am I developing intimacy with Him through crisis times as well as good times?
3. On what basis has the Lord disappointed me? Where in God's Word has He promised these things? Could I be expecting of Him what He didn't promise?
4. What do I know to be true about how God acts on behalf of His children? Do I believe that God won't allow me to face any trial without making a way to endure it? Do I believe He'll give me grace when I need it?
5. Am I separating emotion from faith?

Ask God to grow a heart of faith in you, because you can't do it on your own. Remember that faith is a gift (Eph. 2:8). Go to Him humbly as the disciples did and say, "Lord, increase my faith!" We'll learn more about this next week! "Lord, I believe; help my unbelief!" (Mark 9:24, NKJV).

For days now we've looked at some of the causes and consequences of doubt and the way out of doubt. What it all comes down to is this: Are you going to live by faith or by sight? You need to get off the fence and make a choice.

The same way you come to Christ, by faith, that's how you live for Him. "As you received Christ Jesus the Lord, so walk in him" (Col. 2:6). Every step forward with God is a step of faith. If you can't look back and see the faithfulness of God in your life in the past and trust God with those things in the future, you're going to have a hard time living for Him.

When times are hard and you're not sure what's ahead, you can look back and say, "God is good, and God is faithful. We can wait on Him, and we can trust Him!' Life always has seasons and valleys. Those who walk by faith have confidence that God will bring them out of the wilderness.

Q&A on Doubt

Question. I made the decision to follow Christ five years ago. I want to grow. Others say they can see the fruit of faith in my life, but the doubts creep in so often that I fear I didn't really accept Him. I don't know how my decision could have been more real. How do I get rid of the doubts? Can I know I have accepted Christ when these doubts enter my mind? What could the obstacle be?

Answer. One of the primary ministries of the Holy Spirit is to confirm your relationship with Christ. The Bible talks about two things people do that silence the Holy Spirit's voice. One of them is called "grieving the Holy Spirit." That is where you do things God doesn't want you to do. The Holy Spirit is grieved by your behavior and convicts you about it. When you don't respond to His voice, over time you don't hear or feel His prompting anymore. The second is this: the Bible says not to quench the Holy Sprit by not doing something He is leading you to do (1 Thess. 5:19). Those two things silence the Holy Spirit's voice.

"The Spirit himself bears witness with our spirit that we are children of God" (Rom. 8:16). Often the reason God's children have doubts about their salvation is that they have quieted the confirming voice of the Holy Spirit in their life through sin or failing to do things that God is leading them to do.

Exercise. If this has been or is an issue with you, take a sheet of paper and ask God to reveal anything you need to deal with. Say, "Lord, I have done some things I shouldn't have done, and I have left undone some things You wanted me to do. I have not been obedient. Please show me." As God reveals these things to you, confess them and ask God to cleanse you. As you do that, begin to pray for 30 days, "God, am I your child? God, I need to know for sure." Again, Romans 8:12 promises that the Spirit will bear witness with your spirit that you are the child of God if you remove those hindrances to hearing the Holy Spirit's voice.

Question. What is my responsibility in erasing my doubts? Is it my responsibility or God's to find answers? And how will God reveal my doubts to me?

Answer. You can answer many of these questions in your own walk with the Lord. My experience is that God reveals things to me when I get before Him and open His Word and ask Him to deal with my heart. I say, "I want to know about my doubts and why I am struggling with this thing and what really is holding me back from growing my faith." I can tell you from my experience and the experience of many other believers that God is faithful to answer sincere questions (see Matt. 7:9). If you come before Him and say, "God, I really want to see my faith grow, but I am discouraged about it, and I need to know what the obstacle is. Can you help me discover that? He will. He will reveal it through His Word; through the conviction of His Spirit He will show you what that is. A lot of people could testify to the truth of that.

Question. What does a disappointed doubter do when the disappointment is rooted in God?

Answer. All disappointment with God is related to a wrong understanding of God. You can't understand God rightly and be disappointed with Him. You may wrongly think, *If I do this and that and this, then God will do this. And God promised that if I am a righteous person, I won't struggle or have any hardship.* That is just a lie. Believers and nonbelievers go through the same things. The grace is that nonbelievers go through difficult times without God and believers go through them with God. The irony is that some believers go through tough times without God, too.

God is not taken back by your question; He is not insulted in the least. He knows it is in your heart anyway. Bring those things before Him and say, "God, what is up with this?" Spend some time reading the psalms, and you will see that God encourages probing questions. I believe you will be able to resolve that disappointment with Him.

> I can't see what's in your heart, but you know what's there. Is it doubt or faith? If the Lord has been dealing with you about a specific matter, then you just have to trust Him in that. Tell Him, "I'm facing more than I can handle right now. Lord, increase my faith!"

What the Lord Is Showing Me About Doubt

Check the truths you need to remember in times of doubt.

- ☐ There is a big difference between doubt and disbelief. Doubt questions if God will supply the need.
- ☐ There are difference kinds of doubt—intellectual, disbelief, circumstantial—but one kind of resolve. Look to the Lord whether you see His hand or not.
- ☐ God places regular tests of faith in front of His children. Those tests will shrink or stretch your faith.
- ☐ Doubt sees the obstacles; faith sees the opportunities.
- ☐ When surrounded by doubters, doubting comes easily.
- ☐ God will go a long way in revealing Himself to a person who really wants to believe.
- ☐ Even godly people can be tempted by doubt. The secret is not being tempted long but reviewing God's works and character.
- ☐ A cause of doubt could be grieving and quenching the Holy Spirit.

Lord, thank You for being a good God and faithful God. You see me here with my heart wide open. O God, increase my faith! Please give me a greater capacity to trust You—to rest in Your promises, to sense the reality of who You are. Give me a greater capacity to trust You. Help me to see You related to the circumstances I'm facing—not earthly but eternal things, each one related to my willingness to rest in Your promises and walk closely with You. Grant me that kind of victory. May I be different because of what I've acknowledged here before You. I promise to give You thanks, praise, and glory. In Jesus' name, amen.

WITH AN ATTITUDE OF FAITH

In small groups have fun with name calling! Thomas the disciple will forever be known as Doubting Thomas. Aren't you glad you're not in the Bible and called by your weakest attribute like Angry Adam or Negative Nora? Based on your attitude, what would people nickname you? What nickname would you love to be called?

1. What's the difference between doubt and disbelief?

2. Why were the Israelites frightened to enter the promised land?

3. Do people who have known the Lord a long time doubt?

4. What are the causes and consequences of doubt?

5. Where do you stand regarding doubt and faith?

I Samuel 15:23

Discussion Questions
About Doubt

Video

Aren't you glad to be leaving the wilderness of doubt and moving to the attitude of faith? Watch and listen for what the Bible says about living a life of faith.

Video Notes

__Faith__ is not anti-intellectual.

Faith is active _confidence_ in God.

Faith is not _escapism_.

Faith is not "mind _science_."

Faith is active confidence in God's _word_.

Faith is _believing_ the Word of God.

Faith is believing the Word of God and _acting_ upon it.

Faith is believing the Word of God and acting upon it no matter how I _feel_.

Faith is believing the Word of God and acting upon it no matter how I feel because God promises a good _result_.

1. Name a favorite biblical hero of faith.

2. What is faith?

3. What can you do to have more faith?

4. How important is community in developing your faith?

5. How much faith is enough?

Discussion Questions
About an Attitude of Faith

Study **Challenge** Is your faith weak or strong? Is it crowding out the doubt in your life? This week's study will take a look at people of faith in the Bible and help you apply biblical truths to your life to help you strengthen your faith.

Memory Verse

"Now faith is the assurance of things hoped for, the convictions of things not seen."
Hebrews 11:1

Get a Checkup

As I've been working on my attitudes in my life during this study, I've found an increased sense of the Lord's presence and a joyfulness as I've been shunning those things that lead to wilderness living and embracing those attitudes that lead to promised-land living. Has God been changing you as you've applied these principles from His Word? Have you noticed an increase in joy? or faith? Has the Lord replaced your attitude of complaining, criticizing, coveting, or doubting with gratitude, love, and contentment?

☐ Yes, I've seen changes in these areas of my life:
☐ Not really. I'm kind of coasting through these chapters.

Thanks for your honesty, but I've got to ask, what's holding you back? Without applying these promised-land attitudes, you're likely living in a wilderness in many areas of your life. I know it's hard, and I know it's daily, but as we'll learn in this chapter, without a chosen dependence and trust in the Lord—without faith—life goes nowhere good.

It's not too late to turn around. Tell the Lord right now that you want to live your life through His strength. Left on your own, wilderness attitudes naturally drive your actions, but they don't have to. If you're a child of God, you've got supernatural power available on request. Ask Him right now:

Lord, I want this study to change me by revealing areas of my heart that are holding me back, areas that You want to transform. I know I can't just choose to be different. I need You and Your power to work within my heart. Help me, by faith, to take these final lessons to heart. I invite Your Spirit and Your Word to take root in my heart. Show me where I need Your touch, and help me be willing to walk out of the wilderness and into the promised land. Amen.

What does this mean? It could mean that from here on out you keep these commitments in mind: (Check if you agree.)

☐ I promise to be dissatisfied with anything less than a genuine personal connection with God in these areas of faith (this lesson) and submission (last lesson and final review).
☐ I promise to reflect on the truth I read, do the exercises, even making notes in my Bible so that I can return to this application point in the future.
☐ I promise to give God access to every area of my life.
☐ I promise to ask, "What does this truth mean to me?"
☐ I'll pray, "Lord, I do want You to change my attitude."

Stead income with flexibility (Jehovah-Jireh)

I don't know about you, but as a believer in Jesus Christ and as a pastor, I run into a lot of people who tell me they've "lost" their faith. They just don't believe as they once did.

Do you meet people like this? ☐ Yes ☐ No What do you tell them?

I start by getting right to the heart of their question. I ask them, "What do you think faith is? In whom do you place your faith?" That usually clears things up.

When you share grace and truth with people, you must first get the definition on the table. We'll get to what God's Book says about faith, but let's first rid ourselves of faulty notions about faith.

What do you think faith is?

Faith is not an ostrich, head-in-the-sand denial of the obvious or inevitable. It's not pretending that something is real when deep down you don't believe it. That's fear, not faith.

Faith is not anti-intellectual either. Faith is not a warm feeling that requires you to check your mind at the door. That's feeling, not faith.

Faith is not a stained-glass, dreamy escapism. I cannot live at church, hiding from the real world. That's fluff, not faith.

Faith is not a motivational seminar, with some high-powered guru calling for self-realization, telling you to picture a better future. That's fad, not faith.

Faith is not a positive mental attitude, a you-have-to-keep-believing thing. It's not ignoring pain by embracing optimism. That's foolishness, not faith.

Faith is so integral to the Christian life that it can be boiled down to a practical definition: faith is believing the Word of God and acting upon it, no matter how I feel, because God promises a good result.

Let's break that definition down so you can see how it will work in practical ways in your life.

Faith is believing the Word of God. That word *believing* is not "wouldn't it be nice if …" Believing is a lot more than just shallow hope. Believing is, "I've got all my eggs in one basket. I'm in 100 percent." That's faith. But faith is not believing in a vacuum; it's belief based on the Word of God. That's the key. I'm not trusting the newspaper, the television, my neighbor, or my boss. I believe in a God who wrote a trustworthy Book. "Faith," Romans 10 says, "comes by hearing the Word of God" (see v. 17) so the more I get in God's Book, the greater will be my faith.

Do you believe the Bible is God's Word? ☐ Yes ☐ No ☐ Other
Explain.

Do you believe the Word of God is true? ☐ Yes ☐ No ☐ Other
Explain.

And acting upon it. This is where faith gets feet. Genuine faith always downloads into life. We say we believe in all kinds of things, but we really don't unless it shows up in our lives. In family matters, an active faith means we will trust God to work through a wayward child or even an unbelieving spouse. In finances we will trust God to meet our daily needs while giving tithes and offerings.

> Read 2 Corinthians 9:8.
>
> Ask yourself, *Do I believe that "God is _____ to make all grace abound to you, so that having all _____ in _____, you may abound in every good work"?*

Maybe you're reading this with an overwhelming sense of loneliness. Maybe you're discouraged about your life and your direction. You're not sure where to turn, and you're not sure what to pursue. As a follower of Jesus Christ, you can turn to Him to meet your deepest needs.

When you believe the answers to life's deepest perplexities are found in Christ, then you are believing the Word of God and acting upon it.

> What is your experience? Can you say, "The answer to my deepest life needs is found in Christ"?
> The answer to my financial needs is found in
>
> The answer to my   needs is found in
>
> The answer to my   needs is found in

No matter how I feel. This is critical. Faith discounts how we feel and boldly acts on the Word of God. The question for us is, will I do the thing God has asked me to do and trust God to do the part that only He can do? That's a question of faith. We must choose to obey God even during the times when we don't feel like obeying. Do you ever have times when you don't feel like obeying God's Word? Unless we want to be like roller-coaster Christians for the rest of our lives, we have to get this part down.

Do you have faith to believe that if you would only ask, God would show up and do His work in your heart, your home, your neighborhood, and your church?

Emotions are wonderful. In their rightful place they bring color and fulfillment to our lives. As our servants, emotions can do much good in our lives; but when they become our master and start dictating our actions, we are headed for disaster. Think of your life as a train. Emotions make a lousy engine but a wonderful caboose. Learning this truth has been a real point of victory for me. When I feel frustrated, it doesn't matter how I feel. If I feel anxiety, it doesn't matter how I feel. If I feel like indulging myself, or avoiding a problem, or nursing a personal slight, I must choose to ignore how I feel. I must believe the Word of God and act upon it no matter how I feel. That's faith!

> Can you think of someone whose life is recorded in the Bible who trusted God and believed God's Word and did something in spite of his or her emotions?
>
> Do you have a testimony to the Lord's faithfulness when you believed the Word of God and acted on it no matter how you felt? Record your situation or crisis here.

God promises a good result. Here's the best part of faith: We can act on our faith no matter how we feel because God promises a good result.

Here are four questions I've heard from those struggling with faith:
- Why would I do what God tells me?
- Why would I wait on God to bring my spouse or child to Christ?
- Why would I give of my finances when I have so many debts?
- Why would I invest my energies in following the Lord when I feel like my life is so empty and meaningless?

The answer to each question is the same: because God promises a good result. This message of faith permeates the Bible. Every step with God is a step of faith. Every lesson learned is a lesson of faith. Every victory won is a victory by faith. That's the prominence of faith in God's Book.

Read Hebrews 11:6.
What must a person do when He comes to God?

What is the result for those who diligently seek Him?

What are you trusting God for today?

Do you have faith to believe something that is still unseen right now?
☐ Yes ☐ No

Is it related to ...
☐ your relationship with God?
☐ a spiritual truth you can't seem to grasp
☐ some kind of crisis? A job loss, health loss, relationship loss?
☐ something related to your family and/or kids?
☐ something related to your future?

Do you remember how you felt when you were young and your birthday was coming up? You were so excited. You knew you would get some gifts from your mom and dad, but you also knew there would be some surprises. Birthdays combine assurance and anticipation, and so does faith! Faith is the conviction based on past experience that God will certainly do some things and will have some surprises.

In our last lesson on doubt, we looked at the wavering line between doubt and faith. Does God see our faith "as big as a mustard seed" even when it is surrounded by an ocean of doubt? Yes, God sees our faith, and He moves toward us to help us even when our faith is so small.

What are you trusting God for today? How's your faith?

1	2	3	4	5	6	7	8	9	10
Help me believe, Lord!									Standing strong!

Talk with the Lord about it right now.

WEEK 8. DAY 2. FAITH AND THE CHRISTIAN LIFE

You can't study faith long before you get to Hebrews 11. Hebrews 11 spotlights the lives of men and women who lived with an active confidence in God. This familiar chapter makes obvious the variety of personalities, challenges, and situations yet with the singularity of response: they believed God.

Read Hebrews 11:1-40 to get familiar with this great chapter and answer the following questions.

Hebrews 11:1 says, "Now faith is the assurance of things hoped for, the conviction of things not seen." How do verses 3,7,8,13,27 illustrate the invisible, unseen part of faith? How did people respond to these unseen realities?

What do verses 11-12 say about God?

From verses 23-28, list five insights we have into Moses' background, mind-set, and character that contributed his faith.

How was the result of Moses' and his parents' faith similar? (vv. 23,27)

Though not consistent of their whole trip, what faith response does verse 29 note about the children of Israel?

What physical challenges do you notice people faced?

What emotional challenges?

Why do you think they endured all this?

What phrase in verse 38 describes this group of faith-filled martyrs?

What did they receive on earth for their faith? (v. 39)

Did this surprise you? ☐ Yes ☐ No

What list could you write of people you know or have heard of? For example: By faith, our church is ministering in sacrificial ways to the poor of our community because we want to be obedient to Isaiah 58:7.

By faith,

By faith,

Review our definition of faith:
Faith is _____ the Word of God and _____ upon it no matter how I feel because God promises a _____ result.

Faithful One	Act of Faith	What Was the Good Result?
Abel	Brought a more acceptable offering to God than Cain did	Genesis 4; Hebrews 11:4
Enoch	Was approved as pleasing to God	Genesis 5:21
Noah	Built an ark to save his family from the flood; believed God, who warned him about something that had never happened before	2 Peter 2:5
Abraham	Obeyed when God called him to leave home and go to another land that God would give him as his inheritance; went without knowing where he was going	Exodus 6:8

The Hebrews 11 list of godly men and women illustrates faith in crises and difficult circumstances. Most of these faithful followers did not see God's promises answered in their lifetimes, but they still believed God would do what He had promised. When you look closely at their lives, you don't necessarily see greatness but the sovereign working of God in whom they placed their trust.

Name two or three attributes of God's character that you see illustrated in Hebrews 11.

How do these testimonies inspire you to trust the Lord?

How does Hebrews 12:1-3 follow well after Hebrews 11? Have you ever put those two familiar passages together?

Moses wrote in Psalm 90:1, "Lord, You have been our dwelling place in all generations." People have been trusting God for thousands of years. Contrary to our culture's norm, faith is not a foolish thing to do. God has been faithful not only to generations past but also to you and me personally.

Recall a specific time and place where God has come through for you. How was He faithful? How did He meet your needs?

When you say, I don't know exactly what God is going to do, but I know He's going to do something for my good because I've been trusting Him for a long time, that's the unseen evidence. Don't feel foolish waiting on God to meet your needs. I certainly don't. How many times have I prayed and asked for God to meet my needs, whatever those needs might be? I'll tell you how many—a lot! Why do I keep doing it? Because God has proven Himself faithful.

Faith is active confidence in God. Faith is substance. Faith is evidence. Faith is the power of a vibrant spiritual life. This is found throughout the Bible. " Without faith it is impossible to please [God]" (Heb. 11:6). Faith was the magnet that drew Moses away from the pleasures of Egypt. Faith was the means of Abraham's justification. Faith was the force that overthrew Jericho's wall. Faith was the secret behind Ruth's stirring confession. Faith is the weapon that killed Goliath. Faith was the deciding factor in Elijah's victory on Mount Carmel. Faith is the shield that protected Job in the midst of his trials. Faith was the muzzle that closed the mouth of Daniel's lions.

Lord, thanks for those who have a history of Your faithfulness. I know from their life stories that You bring good results. I pray especially that You will help me remember that You are good and faithful and that You never fail Your children when we obey You by faith. Help me to trust You and see You work in my life. Amen.

Is having faith important? Contrary to the opinion of a lot of sincere people, the answer is no. Faith for faith's sake doesn't go anywhere. Faith doesn't have any magic. Faith in itself doesn't save you, can't help you, doesn't give you anything you need to overcome trials. But faith gets you to God. In fact, faith is the way to everything with God.

Draw a line from the statement to the confirming Scripture reference.

Faith is the way to salvation.	1 Peter 5:8-9
Faith is the way to live your life in God.	2 Corinthians 5:7
Faith is the way to persevere when difficulties come into your life.	Hebrews 11:1
Faith is the way to walk with God.	Acts 16:31
Faith is the way to resist Satan and his attacks.	Galatians 2:20
Faith is the way to please God.	Romans 11:20

Years ago when my kids were younger, I stood on the front porch and called them home for supper. I saw my son a block away hop on his bike and head home. I was so happy to see him that when he got to the front porch and jumped off his bike, I'd run right past him to hug his bike.

That would be silly. But in the same way faith only gets you home. Faith is the vehicle, not the destination. God is fired up by your faith because that's what gets you to Him. People who have faith in Him come to Him. People who don't believe in Him don't come to Him. It's the coming to Him and not the faith itself that pleases God.

Barriers to Faith

What keeps us from believing what God says and acting on it?

Our View of God. In the preface to *The Knowledge of the Holy*, A. W. Tozer wrote, "The decline of the knowledge of the holy has brought on our troubles. A rediscovery of the majesty of God will go a long way toward curing them. It is impossible to keep our moral practices sound and our inward attitudes right while our idea of God is erroneous or inadequate."

In what ways can an incorrect concept of God be a barrier to faith?

Our Addiction to Sight. How can you have faith when you don't see God doing anything? Have you ever had a time in your life when you wondered where God was? "I couldn't see Him working.

I couldn't sense Him. I didn't think He was doing anything." Honestly, have you ever thought that? Everybody's rock solid on God when He unrolls His plans in front of us. The challenge is believing and acting consistently as a believer when we're not seeing it. If you want to grow as a faith-filled follower of Christ, here's what you have to do. You have to break the addiction to sight.

Physically, we walk by sight. The same goes for our spiritual walk. Some of your most discouraging seasons of faith may have been when you said to God, "You say You're this or that, but I'm just not seeing it." God never promised that we would see Him work. God is determined that the life of His follower is a life of faith. Sometimes you'll see His hand; sometimes you won't.

If you wonder if God is at work, what does Hosea 6:3 give as an indication?

What does 2 Chronicles 16:9 say about how God is working out His plan?

Up and down the globe God's eyes search. "Where's the person who's filled with faith? Where's the person in whose life I can work?" Without a doubt God is always at work.

Have you ever been in a tough and challenging place where you doubted if God was working?
☐ Yes ☐ No

I know I have. One time I even had to preach a series called "God @ Work: Even When I'm Not Seeing It" to reinforce my faith in how God works when His plan or timetable isn't matching mine.

God forgive us for the times we have said harshly, "This is way too hard. How could God be in this?" Do you think difficult circumstances prove that God isn't working when, in fact, the Bible says the opposite? That difficult circumstance is not God's pulling back from you; difficult circumstances many times are when God is drawing toward you, embracing and growing you.

What tedium or difficult circumstance do you face today?

Are you trying to figure out where God is? Some of you moms are getting ready for another season with toddlers. Every day the same thing. If I asked you what you are going to do today, you might say, "I'm cleaning up the food the kids spilled at breakfast, and then I'll do the laundry." Listen, God is right in that place!

God is also in that place you work. Some of you carry a heavy burden because you go every day to a job you don't like. You're thinking, *Three million minutes to retirement and counting.* Recently I talked to a man I greatly respect and asked him how it was going at work. He said, "You know, James, my job provides for my family, and it gives me an opportunity to serve God. I don't love it, but I'm thankful for it." He's right on target. God forgive us for thinking that if He's not showing up in some flashy, phenomenal way He's not there working and ordering our steps. God is at work even when we're not seeing it. Acknowledge Him now:

Lord, I know it's true. You're always working. By faith I believe You. Thank You for Your work in my life today. Thank You for Your work in my children and my marriage, even when I'm not seeing it. Thank You for Your work in my church today. Forgive me for needing chills and thrills before I acknowledge Your hand. Teach me what it means to live not by sight but by faith. Help me stand strong by faith. I want to make a covenant with You today, Lord. I want to tell You again that I am Yours; I belong to You; all that I have is Yours. You're everything to me. Help me in these uncertain times to be filled with faith and obedience. Help me today break my addiction to sight and take hold by faith that You are at work, even when I'm not seeing it. Amen.

When we live by faith, we win; and when we live by sight, we lose. If you're a Christian, winning means you have victory over the trials in your life. You remain strong and true to God even when it's tough. It means you are conquering temptation and living without compromise. And it also means not always needing to see the next step before you trust God's Word and follow Him. That's the point I want us to look at now, and there's no better person to study than the man, who "believed God, and it was counted to him as righteousness" (Gal. 3:6).

Biblical Case Study: Abraham

The old patriarch Abraham spent his whole life living out this truth. God drew a major plan for Abraham's family when they were in a land far away from Israel. God said, "I'm starting a new nation, and you're the man I want to head it up. Get up and move over there."

Abraham had a choice. He could have made some good excuses for not moving. They would have sounded a lot like excuses we give for not believing God.

> Name a couple of faithless responses Abraham could have said.

Abraham could have doubted, "Maybe I didn't really hear God right. Maybe I had too much pizza. Maybe it wasn't really God talking to me," and maybe he was just refusing to hear the Word of God.

Abraham could have adapted what God said to make it more conducive to his plans. He could have said, "I know God wants to bless me, but I don't want to move. So I'll just pray, 'Bless me here, God.' I'll live for you here among this pagan people."

Abraham could have delayed. He could have said, "It's not a good time for me to move right now. I'll move later, God, when I see how Your plan plays out."

Abraham didn't do any of these. If he had, he would have lost out on the most incredible plan of the ages that God had designed just for him. Abraham chose instead to live by faith, and he won! Genesis 12:4 says, "So Abram went, as the Lord had told him." That's faith!

Are the choices you're making right now characterized by faith? Are you waiting to see how things go before you step out in faith? Are excuses creeping into your plans? Are you doubting or delaying doing what you know God wants you to do? I'll give it to you straight once again, "When you live by faith, you win; when you live by sight, you lose." Every time.

If you love the Lord with your whole heart and are committed to His purposes, God is at work in your life and your situation. Sometimes you can see what He's doing, and sometimes you can't. When you can't see His hand, trust that He is still at work because You know His character. You believe He will accomplish what He promised. Sometimes we're aware of God's presence, and sometimes God seems far away.

When we think He's distant, it's because we're not yet full circle. A day will come when you will look back and see God's sovereign hand at work in those situations. He is in the center of the situation that troubles your heart right now. Just because you can't see Him doesn't mean He isn't there. Trust Him. He is at work. Have faith.

> What encouragement do you get from Philippians 1:6 and Romans 8:28-29 for your life and for your loved ones?

Faith is one of the most talked topics in the Christian life. The reason we say so much about it is because God's Word says a lot about it. The Greek form of the word *faith* is used 243 times, the verb 249 times, and the adjective form 67 times. It's one of the most common words in the entire New Testament. I typed the word *faith* into my computer search program, asking for references from Romans to Jude—all the letters (epistles). I got 180 references, to say nothing of the synonyms: believing God, trusting God, resting and abiding in Him—all of which contain a significant element of faith. The apostle John said that faith is the victory that overcomes the world (1 John 5:4).

> Believing is a lot more than just shallow hope. Believing is, "I have all my eggs in that place, I'm 100 percent in, and I don't have an escape route." That's faith.

Faith was constantly on Jesus' mind as He ministered and lived His life on earth. Jesus said: "If you have faith like a grain of mustard seed, you will say to this mountain, 'Move from here to there,' and it will move" (Matt. 17:20). "Whatever you ask of the Father in my name, he will give it to you" (John 16:23). Jesus often rebuked the disciples when they failed with the phrase, "O you of little faith" (Matt. 6:30; 8:26; 14:31; 16:8; 17:20; Luke 12:28). All of this begs the question: faith in what?

Faith in faith? No, that's a cultic message in the power of faith itself. I'm sure you've heard it everywhere. "Crank up your faith." "Just believe!" That false teaching is on television every day. The Bible doesn't teach that there's power in your faith. There's no power in what you say or do or your posture or your positive outlook on life. But there is power in God's Word. And if what you believe is God's Word, and what you act on is God's Word, that's where the power is to live a victorious life in Christ. A lot of people are trusting in good works to get them to heaven. Sadly that's not going to make it. It's what you have faith in that makes a difference.

King David summed it up well in Psalm 20:7: "Some trust in chariots and some in horses, but we trust in the name of the Lord our God." True faith is not a matter of personal strength, not an issue of how much faith we have, not a question of how much certainty we can muster to meet our needs. Biblical faith, rather, is dependence on the Person in whom we claim to believe. The key to a life of faith lies in focusing our attention on God, our Source, instead of on the answers to our prayers. True faith focuses not on our ability to believe but on the character of God. The Hebrews 11 faith heroes were not highlighted for the strength or quantity of their faith but for their focus on the Lord. The next chapter says that they fixed their eyes on the unseen Lord, the "founder and perfecter of our faith" (v. 2). Following their lead, if we want to build our faith on the only lasting foundation, we'll learn to focus on the greatness of God.

> All things are possible in Christ. He's promised to do so much more for us if we just believe Him. That's what the Word of God teaches. That's not just for another age; that's for us today as the followers of Jesus Christ.

Case Study: Faith Building

It wasn't a familiar mood to me, but I was depressed, and I knew it. I had just finished the school year, teaching seventh-grade science, and I was exhausted. As I looked back over the year, I saw nothing but failure.

What an unproductive, futile year, I thought. I decided to go for a ride in the countryside. When I came upon a particularly beautiful scenic overlook, I stopped the car, got out, and stood by the edge of the cliff—not to jump but just to get perspective! For some reason God's words to Abraham came to mind, "In you all the families of the earth shall be blessed" (Gen. 12:3). I recalled learning that blessing springs from faith. I laughed at the thought of me blessing anyone. Immediately countering that thought, I sensed God's Spirit prompting me, "Are you going to believe your feelings or My Word?" Then He gave me faith to believe Him.

What did this discouraged teacher do right?

How does this show the value of our definition, "Faith is believing the Word of God and acting upon it no matter how I feel because God promises a good result"?

We don't know the end of this testimony, but what do you think happened next?

Nothing Has Nothing to Do with Faith

Huh? Read that again. You might be well into this study of attitudes, but you're thinking, *This faith thing is great. God, faith, super. But it doesn't have a whole lot to do with the problems I'm facing right now. I've got some personal problems. I've got some burdens. I've got some struggles that do not have anything to do with faith.*

Listen, friend. Nothing has nothing to do with faith. Stop compartmentalizing your life. Almighty God wants to be absolutely central in every single subject matter of your life. Don't have a separate drawer for the God things, OK? Faith is about everything you're facing. You couldn't possibly have a burden that doesn't have faith as the central subject matter. But it will require your getting with God in a quiet, uninterrupted place and asking Him to show you what you need to do to receive His grace for your situation.

Begin by saying, "Lord, here is my need."

I love to go camping. My favorite place is Algonquin Park in northern Ontario, Canada. It has hundreds of square miles of wilderness without electricity or running water. You're not even allowed to take cans or bottles into the park. At night the park gets so dark you can't even see your hand in front of your face so we always take a really good flashlight.

Now imagine me stumbling down some wilderness trail in the night. Imagine I have my flashlight with me, but for some reason I refuse to switch it on. Imagine that I stumble around for hours getting eaten by mosquitoes and scraping my legs.

"What a waste," you say. "All you had to do to spare yourself the frustration was to turn on the flashlight; just flip the switch!" Right! What a waste to have all this Bible knowledge yet walk around in the dark because you don't turn on the power through the Holy Spirit. Exercise some faith! Faith is the switch that turns on the power of the Holy Spirit.

"For indeed the gospel was preached to us as well as to them; but the word which they heard did not profit them, not being mixed with faith in those who heard it" (Heb. 4:2, NKJV). This truth applies to far more than just the gospel. The way we come to Christ is also the way we follow Him: "As you therefore have received Christ Jesus the Lord, so walk in Him" (Col. 2:6, NKJV) Every step with God is a step of faith.

> *Knowledge of the Word by itself is not enough, we must exercise our faith in the truth of God's Word.*

We're learning a lot in this study of attitudes, but if you don't combine all that you're learning with faith, it will make absolutely no difference in your life. Unless you exercise your faith in regard to these truths, you will not be changed! You may understand a lot about how to change according to God's plan, yet you will not change. We all know people who have a head full of Bible information but aren't anything like Christ. It's not about knowing the truth; it starts with knowing, but it doesn't end there. You have to take what you know and combine that truth with faith.

I like the NIV translation of Hebrews 4:2: "The message they heard was of no value to them, because those who heard did not combine it with faith." You are not different because you know; you're different because you choose to live and act by faith. Unless you add faith to the truths you're learning, this study will prove ultimately useless to you.

I don't know if you've ever been to a desperate place—like where your need was great, where the time was short, and where the options were zero. It could be a health crisis, a devastating financial reversal, a vicious personal problem or assault, a moral collapse, or an emotionally shattering event. If you've ever been in a desperate place, then you know what it's like to wonder from the depth of your soul, "How do I get God to help me?"

When we last met the children of Israel in our study, they were in this place. Time after time they stood on the cliff with no way out, but each time God provided, protected, and brought them to safety. Problem was, their memory was short, and they doubted His character each time.

If you're not at a place of desperation, you will be at some point in your life, and you're going to need the truth we're going after today. How do I access God at that time of desperation in my life? What can I do to move God to respond? There are ways. Let's get it on the table.

What Makes Faith Stronger?

Get into God's Word. Romans 10:17 says, "Faith comes by hearing, and hearing by the word of God" (NKJV). When Jesus taught on this, He said, "The wise man was the one who heard the Word of God and did it" (see Luke 11:28). Biblically speaking, hearing is hearing and doing. The biggest fool of all is the person who hears but doesn't do.

Has there been a time when you've heard the Word of God taught and felt your faith welling up within you? ☐ Yes ☐ No

God's <u>Word</u> gives faith. If you're filled with doubt, the first thing I'd ask you is, "How much time are you spending in God's Word?" If you want faith, memorize God's Word, meditate on God's Word, devote yourself to reading and studying God's Word, and you'll have greater faith.

I love the truth that's in the Bible. It's God's heart for us; and when we wash our minds with it daily and continuously, it produces faith within us. When we fill our minds with the headlines, the latest worldly romance, and more television and other entertainment, no wonder we struggle with faith. We fill our days and our ears with everything but the Word of God, and so we lack the faith to obey. Romans 12:2 teaches that our transformation comes by the "renewing of your mind" (NIV), and that comes from immersing ourselves in God's Word.

If we could stick a thermometer under your tongue and measure the level of your faith, the thing that would cause your faith's temperature to go up immeasurably is the minutes, hours, and days that you've spent with your nose in God's Word.

As you study the temptations in Matthew 4, you can't help but notice that Jesus used faith in the Word of God as His only basis for victory. When tempted to turn stones into bread, Jesus said, "Man shall not live by bread alone, but by every word that proceeds from the mouth of God" (v. 4, NKJV), quoting Deuteronomy 8:3.

When tempted to throw Himself down (see vv. 6-7), Jesus answered, "It is written again, 'You shall not tempt the Lord your God,'" quoting Deuteronomy 6:16. When Satan offered "all the kingdoms of the world … if You will … worship me" (vv. 8-9), Jesus said, "Away with you, Satan! For it is written, 'You shall worship the Lord your God, and Him only you shall serve'" (v. 10), this time quoting Deuteronomy 10:20.

Three temptations. Three biblical answers. What a perfect example of the power of faith in God's Word.

Confess your faith. Ephesians 6:19-20 says, "Also for me, that words may be given to me in opening my mouth boldly to proclaim the mystery of the gospel, for which I am an ambassador in chains, that I may declare it boldly, as I ought to speak."

Have you ever had an experience where you were somewhat discouraged spiritually until all of a sudden God gave you an opportunity to speak for Him and share your faith? ☐ Yes ☐ No

Tell about it here.

Exercise. Faith is like a muscle; it gets stronger with use. When you commit yourself, "I'm going to trust God in this. I'm not going to meddle in it. I'm going to leave it with Him" and then step out and trust God, your faith grows. This will create experience in faith walking. The longer you live, the more you see the goodness and faithfulness of God. Let's care for little believers who don't have a lot of experience yet. Let's let the experience of God's faithfulness build our faith.

Tell a story about how God brought you through something that built your faith.

What are you doing that puts you in a position where you have to trust God?

Practice genuine prayer. The kind of prayer I'm talking about is on-your-knees-before-God heartfelt prayer, laying hold of God by faith. You ask, "I'm not very good at that. Is there a seminar I can go to?" Yes, it's conducted daily in your home in a private place where you can kneel down. It's given by the Holy Spirit and available to you 24-7. The way to learn how to pray is to say, "Lord, teach me to pray."

The power of prayer to build faith is phenomenal. I have experienced this many times in my life. When I'm filled with anxiety or concerns and burdens, I remember, "Pray!" So I get by myself and kneel down in humility before God; and in the simplest language I know, I talk with my Father about my needs. Every time I do, it isn't long at all before my genuine heartfelt prayer leads me to get up off my knees, feeling those burdens lifted, and knowing that my anxiety has been replaced by faith.

If you want the power to change, it can only come through the Holy Spirit. The Holy Spirit pours on the power in response to your faith! You might begin by asking as the apostles did, "Lord, increase our faith" (see Luke 17:5).

I love what Jesus said in Luke 22:32: "Peter, I have prayed for you that your faith would not fail." I don't want my faith to fail, either. Pray. Pray. And remember Jesus is praying for you.

Take a moment to think about what the next three days will be like for you. Write down the major challenge you will face each day, then a verse reference to show how faith in God's Word will intersect that challenge and help you to experience victory.

Day 1 Challenge

God's Word says

Day 2 Challenge

God's Word says

Walk faithfully. I want to give everything I have to walk faithfully with the Lord until that final moment when I go to take another step and I step into heaven. That's what I want to do. I want to walk faithfully with God for a lifetime. You too?

I want to stay on that path. I don't want to get off of it. If you've ever been off the path, you know there's nothing good about being in a ditch. I don't want to be a casualty. I can't be perfect, but I can be faith filled.

Do you believe that God rewards those who walk faithfully with Him for a lifetime? Sometimes when we think about the Christian life, we think about the ways it can fulfill us here and now, but I believe the greatest part about living the Christian life is what's ahead. I believe that by faith, and it's keeping me going. Come with me, and let's catch up with Paul so we can say with him, "I have fought the good fight, I have finished the race, I've kept the faith" (2 Tim. 4:7).

What the Lord Is Teaching Me About Faith

1. Faith is believing the Word of God and acting on it no matter how I feel because God has promised a good result.
2. Faith is not part of the Christian life; it's the whole thing.
3. Faith is what gets us to God.
4. Abraham's faith took him to a new place and to a new place with God.
5. True faith is rooted in God's character.
6. Faith is the switch that turns on the power of the Holy Spirit.

REPLACE A REBELLIOUS ATTITUDE ...

Discuss in small groups. Name some things in your everyday life that you depend on even though you can't see them. How is faith like and different from these other daily invisibles?

1. How meaningful is this study to you? Are you changing?

2. How does Hebrews 11 illustrate faith using people from the Old Testament?

3. What barriers keep you from God?

4. In what should you have faith?

5. How can faith increase?

I Sam. 15:23

Discussion Questions
About Faith

Rom. 13:1

Video

Korah means bald one

We're going back to the desert one last time with a rebellious attitude. This one is really serious. Watch and see if you are a rebel and how you can change from your rebellious ways. Listen for truths from God's Word.

Video Notes

Rebellion is serious. Numbers 16   Korah's Rebellion

Those who choose murmuring as their **lifestyle** will spend their lifetime in the wilderness.

Rebellion exists in every human **heart**. Number 16:1-2

Rebellion is **Knowing** but not doing what God wants you to do.   Proverbs 22:15

Rebellion has many **sources**.

Rebellion has many sources

Six Sources of Rebellion

1. Jealousy Num. 16:3
2. Delusions v. 4; 5-7 (about themselves.) people have delusions
3. Ungratefulness v. 8-11
4. Stubbornness v. 12
5. Disappointment v. 13-14
6. Distrust

Rebellion has many Consequences

Consequences of Rebellion Num. 16:15-22

1. Leadership withdrawal
2. Innocence defiled Num. 16: 25-27
3. Guilty condemned v. 28-30
4. Infection spreads v. 30-35

Rebellion is ultimately against God.

Numbers 16:11   v: 36-40

Number 16:41-46

1. What is rebellion?

2. How were the Hebrew people rebellious?

3. Which Scripture was most meaningful to you about a rebellious attitude?

4. Which source of rebellion do you see most often?

5. Which consequence of rebellion do you think poses the greatest threat?

Discussion Questions
About Rebellion

Study   **Challenge**   In this last trip to the wilderness, consider where rebellion will take you and what you'll need to change to enjoy promised-land living.

Free me from a rebellious heart

Memory Verse

"There is a way that seems right to a man, but its end is the way to death."
Proverbs 16:25

Not one of us could say, "I may struggle with other attitudes, but the attitude of rebellion just isn't a problem for me." Some may not know what to call it, but we must all acknowledge that at the core of our being we want to be in charge, and we get downright angry when we're not.

I'm sure Frank Sinatra didn't know when he sang his ballad "My Way" that he was capturing the theme song for rebellious people of all time. Some might say, "Well, that's just independence or strong self-assurance." Right. At its core rebellion says, "I don't need God. I will do it my way; and if pushed to do it another's way, including God's, I will just say no. So whether the person is a 2-year-old child being asked to pick up her toys, a teenage son being told what time to be home, someone driving without wearing a seatbelt, or someone refusing to trust the Lord, the end result is rebellion. And that is a dangerous, deadly slope, especially with God.

Today is our last trip to the desert. It's one of the darkest days in the 38 years in the wilderness. Twice God wanted to wipe out all of the people because of their outrageously bad attitudes. Only in His mercy and with Moses' pleading for them did they survive. What's particularly frightening is that they didn't seem to learn; and as we've learned throughout this study, we're not so different from them. The issue is rebellion. God says this; we want that. God has placed human authority levels over each of us, and we don't like it. That exists in every human heart, and it's serious. You may ask, "Why are we rebellious? What is the source of rebellion? Where does rebellion lead? How can I change?" These are the questions we'll go after today.

Identify with an X the situations you think include rebellion.

_____ 1. Two friends are fighting. One wants to make up; the other doesn't.

_____ 2. Your boss is an idiot. Why should you knock yourself out on a report to make him look good?

_____ 3. Your teenage girl abides by your dress code (until she changes her outfit at school).

_____ 4. You're late for an important meeting. The speed limit is 45.

_____ 5. Your church takes sides in a conflict regarding the pastor. A split is on the horizon.

_____ 6. How many times has your spouse worked late this week? Now he wants time together?

_____ 7. In the year since your mother died, it's been hard to be as enthusiastic about your Bible study group as you used to be.

_____ 8. Since you didn't get the promotion at work, you say you can't afford to keep up your tithe the way you used to.

_____ 9. The last time God answered a specific prayer is a dim memory.

_____ 10. You find yourself critiquing the sermon rather than listening for what you can learn and apply in your own life.

_____ 11. You're not really sure that you love God or that God loves you.

_____ 12. Those smiling, happy Christians really get on your nerves.

Meanwhile, Back in the Desert

We don't know where or when during the 38 years of wandering pure rebellion took place in Israel, but we do know who and why.

Read Numbers 16:1-2.

Who were the ringleaders of this rebellion?

How many people were involved?

These were some of the most respected priests in the entire society. What was their accusation?

Rebellion against proper authority reveals a deeper rejection of God's authority, which brings devastating consequences to our lives.

What do you see as the real motive?

Read Numbers 16:3-11.

Paraphrase Moses' response.

How did jealousy prompt Korah's rebellion?

Do you think Korah understood what it would take to lead God's people?

What was Korah ungrateful for (Num. 16:9-11)?

What advantage is it to rebels to get into a group to stir up trouble?

Read Numbers 16:12-15.

How did Dathan and Abiram's response to Moses reveal their disappointment?

What was their level of trust in Moses?

Read Numbers 16:19-22.

What did God command Moses and Aaron to do with these men?

Read Numbers 16:25-35.

In your best "television teaser language" describe what happened next.

Step Away from the Tents

How were the innocent affected by this rebellion (Num. 16:27)?

What happened to the guilty (Num. 16:28-35)?

After seeing an obviously divine judgment, how did the people respond the next day (Num. 16:41)?

What did they accuse Moses of doing?

What did Moses say about the rebellion (Num. 16:11)?

Contrary to what most people might think, God-given authority is like an umbrella in our lives. It's a protection against a lot of hurt in this world. Although God allows some in our lives, He protects us from much of what would hurt us by placing us under authority. No authority is perfect, but the powers that be are ordained of God. Unless they're asking you to sin, you need to do what you're asked to do. To choose not to obey is to place yourself in a position of great risk. Think about your life. How much pain have you experienced due to the bad decisions you've made to get out from under worthy authority and the consequences that you reap—sometimes for the rest of your life?

Since the beginning, the sovereign Lord of the universe has held out His hand to direct His children in the way they should go. But like a child pulling his hand away from his parent's on a busy street, we've disregarded the wise instructions and have turned every one to his own way. Generation after generation, this rebellion has turned ugly, hurting every relationship and outcome. This has resulted in our doing what's right in our own eyes and missing God's plan for our good and fruitful lives. We can't be thankful; we can't worship; we can't be content. When we go our own way, we forget the concept of God's sovereignty and walk a line much more dangerous than we think.

Review these familiar stories of the Old Testament from the perspective of our natural-born rebellious ways, rejecting God's authority and the human institutions He has established for our good and protection. Look over these four examples of rebellion: Lucifer, Adam, Saul, and Jonah. What conclusions can you draw about the consequences of a rebellious heart?

Lucifer—Angel of Light Becomes Satan, Prince of Darkness

Before God spoke creation into existence, a war of wills was happening in heaven. Read Isaiah 14:12-16 to overhear the rebellious statements Lucifer made before our time began. He claimed:

> "I will ascend to _____; above the _____ of God.
> I will set my _____ on high;
> I will _____ on the mount of assembly in the far reaches of the north;
> I will ascend above the heights of the clouds;
> I will make _____ like the Most _____."

Where will Lucifer end up? See verses 15-16.

Adam and Eve: Kicked Out of Eden

Read Genesis 3. God told Adam and Eve, "Here's the whole world I've created. Go where you want; eat what you want. But there's one thing you can't do."

What did they do?

What happened next?

Rebellion involves knowing what God wants you to do and refusing to do it.

Saul: Going Down

What you do when you're confronted about your own sin is one of the most critical things in your life. That is the great dividing line in all of humanity. When Samuel pointed Saul's rebellion out to him, Saul refused to see it, admit it, or repent of it. Read about the final straw in King Saul's rebellious spiral in 2 Samuel 15:12-23.

How did Saul rebel in this passage?

How did he rationalize his sin?

What was God's response?

Jonah: Running from God

Read Jonah 3:10-4:4. It wasn't that he was afraid for his life. It wasn't that he thought he would be ineffective. Jonah refused God's instructions to go to Nineveh on principle. God's compassion would show mercy to this wicked people, and Jonah hated that thought. So when God told Jonah to go east, he went west as fast as he could.

What does this say about God's character toward rebellious people (in Nineveh) who turn back to God?

Had Jonah gotten over his rebellious attitude by the time he went to Nineveh?

A Long Time Since Eden: Rebellion's Consequence

The soap bubbles couldn't hold up much longer, but neither could she. First her glass, then her plate, and finally the spaghetti pot. Layer upon layer of white clouds melted into the muddy-red dishwater. And still Eve stood there, wringing out her rag, wiping the faucet, dodging the tears disrupting the now flat, filthy water.

Turning from the sink, she cleared the table, picked up the plate still piled with pasta, and sealed it tight with plastic wrap. She made room for it in the fridge beside last night's leftovers. Tomorrow another plate will replace yesterday's. She had come to expect it, but that didn't keep her from hoping, didn't keep her from listening for the crunch of his wheels on the gravel or turning at every sound in the hall.

Once they had been happy. Embossed in her memory was the way he had looked at her, like they were the only lovers in the world. When he held her that first time, he had whispered, "I found you!" And now she can't find him, only the shadow of the man she once knew. He's distant, caught up in a dream of a far-off place. She remembered that place, too—a paradise that was their choice to forfeit.

Leaving the porch light on, Eve climbed the stairs. The decades-old question echoed on each step. What if? What if? What if? Their guilt and blame had long been silenced. Their quest for independence from God was costly, so expensive that the payments stretched over a lifetime.

Eve stared at the bedroom ceiling with a magazine propped unread in her lap. Adam sat in the car down the street, listening to the canned laughter coming from the neighbor's TV and waiting for their bedroom light to go out.

What does this vignette illustrate as the personal cost of rebellion against God?

How does rebellion harm horizontal relationships as well as our vertical relationship with God?

Have you witnessed or experienced the personal consequences of knowing what God wants you to do and doing your own thing instead? ☐ Yes ☐ No

What are the short-term and long-term results?

What needs to be done to resolve the rebellion?

Can the consequences be avoided? ☐ Yes ☐ No

The scenarios that could be reported here are varied and numerous. But here's the common denominator: You want it to be this way; God's Word says it should be another way. Will you choose God's way or your own? The situations could be public, as in family or church issues; personal, as in how you spend your time or money; or private, whether you will trust the Lord in times of crisis or pressure. The wisdom of your choice will determine to a great extent the direction of your life. How many of us have lived for years with the fallout of rebellion? God gives sustaining grace, but the consequences continue. God helps us increasingly desire His way—no matter what.

Defining Pride

Pride is the root of every sin, especially the sin of rebellion. Check out this dictionary definition of *pride*: "inordinate self-esteem, an unreasonable conceit of one's own superiority; insolence; rude treatment of others; personal exaltation; a generous elation of the heart; noble self-esteem springing from a consciousness of your own worth; an elevated opinion of self." Now compare that definition with what Paul had to say in Romans 12:3: "By the grace given to me I say to everyone among you not to think of himself more highly than he ought to think, but to think with sober judgment, each according to the measure of faith that God has assigned."

What is the fundamental difference?

Read Romans 1:18-23. What do these verses say about rebellion?

What authority structure has God ordained for your life?
Look up the Scriptures and name the human authority.

Romans 13:1-7

1 Timothy 3:8-11; 1 Peter 5:5

Ephesians 5:21-24

Ephesians 6:1

Ephesians 6:5-8

"Obey your leaders and submit to them, for they are keeping watch over your souls, as those who will have to give an account. Let them do this with joy and not with groaning, for that would be of no advantage to you."
—Hebrews 13:17

Are You a Rebel?

Are you difficult to lead? Don't answer this question without praying about it first.

1. Ask the Lord to bring to mind the faces of specific people whose rightful authority you have resisted.
2. Invite the Holy Spirit to examine each of the relationships in your life: family, marriage, work, the body of Christ. Are you playing the rebel's role in any of those places?
3. Have you realized that your heart has been like a wilderness because your life has the undeniable symptoms of rebellion?

Lord, I confess to You that my heart has not been right toward _____. I have stiffened my neck at their authority. I don't know if this has been obvious to them or to others, but I know You haven't missed it. I sincerely repent of _____ right now. Please replace this rebellious attitude with Your Spirit. Fill me anew with _____. I know that every rebellious act is ultimately against You.

I want to talk to you practically about the attitude of rebellion. How does it happen? What should you do if you see rebellion in your own heart?

If you've been around the church for long, you've noticed that all God's children experience seasons of training. Some people are sweetened by trials, and some people get bitter and angry. From some people the season of discipline kicks in their spiritual pride. *I shouldn't be treated this way.* Others lose sight of the long obedience in the same direction and think that God has deserted them.

Today I want us to look at why some people's hearts turn rebellious and refuse to learn what God is trying to teach them through their season of discipline. Sooner or later this season hits us all so it's good to be prepared for your turn.

When you stand up against God, you're not going anywhere good.

Step 1. Discipline Leads to Discouragement

What happened to Bill? You know, that guy who used to come to church and carry his Bible and was all fired up about the Lord? Now he doesn't want anything to do with God. He's not going to church; and if you try to talk with him, he gets upset if you bring up anything about the Lord.

Discipline is a painful circumstance allowed by God to transform a person's conduct and character. The word *discipline* in Hebrews 12 can be interchanged with *training*. Discipline should not be understood as punishment since Jesus paid the punishment for our sin by His sacrifice on the cross.

Read Hebrews 12:5-11.

Why do you think people get discouraged while in training?

Do you think a rebellious attitude has set in for Bill?　☐ Yes　☐ No

Explain your answer.

Why are we disciplined? See verse 11.

What would you say to someone who rebels against the training?

What are the signs of discouragement according to Hebrews 12:12-13?

Why would God's training lead some to discouragement and others to greater faith?

What wrong attitudes could kick in?

The Lord's discipline can lead to discouragement, but it doesn't have to. You can embrace it instead. You can experience God's strength instead.

According to 2 Corinthians 12:9, when is God's strength made perfect?

When you get hold of what you're supposed to be learning, whatever it is—to trust more, to follow more closely, to reorganize your priorities—the discipline of the Lord does not have to lead to discouragement. But it can.

Step 2. Discouragement Leads to Dislocation

This is a lot more serious. Hebrews 12:13 says, "Make straight paths for your feet, so that what is lame may not be put out of joint but rather be healed." If you've ever turned your ankle, you know it's not good to be dislocated physically. Being dislocated spiritually is also painful. Why do you get dislocated? Because pressure comes at the wrong angle. Think about God's hands pressuring you, trying to teach you something. The dislocation comes when you try to get out from under it. God's trying to get your attention and get something through to you. If a rebellious attitude kicks in, you could dislocate your life spiritually. Discipline can lead to discouragement. Discouragement leads to dislocation.

Step 3. Dislocation Leads to Bitterness

"See to it that no one fails to obtain the grace of God; that no 'root of bitterness' springs up and causes trouble, and by it many become defiled" (Heb. 12:13). Notice that phrase, "fails to obtain the grace of God." Do you know that God gives grace in His training? Have you seen someone go through a difficult season and you've thought, *I could never go through what they're going through?*

◯ **Yes** ◯ **No** Recall the situation.

What you don't know is that God is giving them grace sufficient for their trial. How much grace? Enough.

No matter what you face, no matter what discipline you go through, no matter what training you experience, no matter what hardship or trial God allows, no matter what refining furnace He runs you through, no matter how high the waters get, they will not overwhelm you. God's grace will be enough for you if you draw down upon it.

You make the choice to avoid a rebellious spiral. When God puts the pressure on, if you fail to learn the thing that God's trying to teach you and you don't submit to Him and draw down upon His grace, the situation can get ugly fast. When God allows a trial, choose to be trained by the discipline of the Lord. Turn to Him for His grace. Or turn rebellious and begin growing a root of bitterness.

Back in the desert, we read in Deuteronomy 29:18: "Beware lest there be among you a man or woman … whose heart is turning away today from the Lord, to go and serve the gods of those nations. Beware lest there be among you a root bearing poisonous and bitter fruit." Bitterness is independence. I can do this on my own. I can get through this. I don't have to learn. If you slap away the good hand of the Lord, you're going to grow a root of bitterness, the pain of heart caused by living apart from His grace. It's the medicine of God gone sour. It's the wounded, unattended, infected, foul-smelling heart that refuses the Lord's training.

Bitterness starts off as a root—underground. Nobody can see it. Like a root it grows shoots around your heart and strangles your love for God and your victory and your joy, and all the good things in the Christian life get choked out. Then bitterness springs up. If you think the root is bitter, wait until you see the tree. It's ugly.

What is the result of bitterness, according to verse 15?

Where is bitterness felt most?

What would be the safe response for people at this step in the spiral to rebellion?

How much trouble in the home is the result of a bitter person?

How much trouble in a church is the result of bitter people who won't learn what God wants them to learn?

> Let the cool breeze of God's grace blow across your spirit and heal your discouragement because you're learning what God wants you to learn. You're submitting to Him. That's a phenomenal place to be.

Step 4. Bitterness Leads to Profane Living

Profane living, as illustrated by the mention of Esau in verse 15, is the attitude of "God means nothing to me! I want what I want. I want to go where I want to go, and I want to say what I want to say. I want to see what I want to see, and I want to experience what I want to experience."

Eventually you come to the place where you say, "I don't really care what God wants or says or thinks. When I say no to God and yes to myself, to my comfort, my pleasure, my desires, He steps toward me with some painful something with the promise of an education." A rebellious, profane person says, "No, I won't." You can say no to God for a bit and just be discouraged. You can say no to God for a while and be dislocated. But if you say no to God for an extended period of time, you're going to become bitter. If you say, "No, God, not now, not ever," eventually you're going to become a profane person. Profane living is the picture of ultimate rebellion against God.

James's High School Reunion

Early in my high school years I was a rebel. I did things I'm not proud of and lived on the wrong side of the message that I've preached to you. Painfully, God had to break me of a lot of attitudes. So when a high school reunion was announced, I thought, *This is my chance to share the gospel with my old crowd that I haven't seen for more than 25 years.*

The reunion was held at a bar; and by the time we got there, most of the people were half in the bag already. They talked to me about "the old days" all the while cursing and swearing. Inevitably the question was asked, "So what are you doing now?" and I said, "I'm a fully devoted follower of Jesus Christ and a minister of the gospel." I had the perfect opportunity to share the transforming power of the gospel. We stayed there pretty late, talking and answering questions.

It was so sad to see people locked in time. They had the same beer in their hand as they did 25 years ago. They were just a little wider in the face, a little redder in the eyes, and a little sadder about the future. They were living profane lives.

Rebellion is the complete state of anti-God, and it goes nowhere good. The only thing God can't overcome, because He won't overcome, is your rebellious will.

Lord, call us off the downward spiral of refusing Your discipline. Give us humility and submissive spirits. O God, teach us what You want us to learn and teach us soon. Drill it deeply into our lives that we might be transformed from glory to glory and honor You. Lord, we don't understand all that You allow. We want to honor You with the trials we face. Lord Jesus, have Your way. We surrender all of our ambitions, hopes, and plans into Your hands. Keep our hearts soft, we pray. In Jesus' name, amen.

We're almost at the end of our study. How are you doing with your attitude? Are you experiencing any change?

A confidence that I have every week when I teach God's Word is that its effectiveness in changing the hearts of the listeners has extremely little, if anything, to do with me, my words, my style or skill, my content. That's also true for this Bible study. I take great comfort in that. My responsibility as a Bible teacher and pastor is to tell you that this is what God said and to help you obey Him. I understand where the hurdles are in the Christian life. I hope to run alongside you who are faithful and want to please God, to whisper courage to you and help you persevere, and to help others who have lost their way to get back on the path. That's my only job. The job of transformation belongs to you and the Lord—your willingness, His power.

Last week we studied that faith comes from hearing God's Word. That's where the power to change comes from—God's Word and God's Spirit. You've come a long way so far in our study and read a ton of Scripture. But have you heard the Spirit's voice or felt His prompting you to change? If you can say, "Yes, I'm seeing my attitudes turning toward what pleases God," then I'm so glad and want to encourage you to keep going. This is an answer to my prayer as well as everyone who has worked on this project.

If you have gone through this study faithfully and have not experienced any change or growth, I think I know what the problem is. It involves this whole subject of who is in charge of your life.

Is trust easy or hard for you?

Have you had disappointing relationships with people that have caused you to choose to rely entirely on yourself? ☐ Yes ☐ No

How do you think this affects your willingness to let God take charge of your life?

If you can look to a time when you surrendered your life to Jesus Christ, acknowledged your sin and your need for a Savior, turned around from following your own plans and strategies to have your own way, and received God's gift of eternal life, then you are a child of God who perhaps has gotten off track. You're in the family, but your heart has been far from God. Good for you for picking up this study. Did you hope this was the answer to this distance you feel from God?

The truth of the matter is that you don't need to work on your attitude as much as you need to get your relationship right with the Lord. You may have been doing your own thing for so long that there's a truckload of stuff in the way, and you're not hearing the Spirit's voice anymore. Do what it takes to get back in a right relationship with God. Don't be rebellious and wish it could be different or easier.

When the author of Hebrews was writing his letter to believers, he referenced the passage we are studying this week—Numbers 16. He wrote in Hebrews 3:7-8, "Therefore, as the Holy Spirit says, 'Today, if you hear his voice, do not harden your hearts as in the rebellion.' " Soften your heart to how He is drawing you to Himself. God loves you, and He's provided the way for your relationship with Him to be restored.

Or maybe you've realized so far in this study that you've always tried to make your way in life on your own. You've been operating on a self-improvement plan, and all that you've read in this study is just another way to have a better life. I know that you know that plan isn't working. It may look like it on the outside, but deep down you're searching for an illusive peace with God. I'm glad to tell you that what you're longing for is available to you. Millions of people down through history have found a satisfying, peace-filled, joy-filled relationship with God that eclipses every satisfaction anyone could know. That relationship begins with this question: what are you going to do with the sin in your heart that blocks you from God? All of the talk about God having a wonderful plan for your life is true, but it must begin here.

If you've been working on a self-improvement plan, how is that going?

Have you ever thought of your self-reliance as rebellion against God? ☐ Yes ☐ No

How would your thinking have to change to let God take the lead in your life?

We've talked about rebellion in this chapter. Rebellion is basically telling God, "I can make it without You." That is a lie. Remember that Sinatra hit, "My Way"? That song is sung in hell today. Your way takes you to that one place. But it doesn't have to be that way for you. Ready for the good news?

God loves you and wants to have a personal relationship with you—now and for all eternity. Jesus said, "I came that they may have life and have it abundantly" (John 10:10). And He said, "For God so loved the world, that he gave his only Son, that whoever believes in him should not perish but have eternal life" (John 3:16).

All of us have rebelled against God and are separated from a relationship with Him. God's Word calls this rebellion "sin." Sin is doing what we want instead of what God wants—in thought, word, or deed. All of us have sinned against God either by doing what He says we should not do or by not doing what He says we should do. "None is righteous, no, not one; no one understands; no one seeks for God. … For all have sinned and fall short of the glory of God" (Rom. 3:10,23). "So whoever knows the right thing to do and fails to do it, for him it is sin" (Jas. 4:17).

Even the good things that we do don't measure up to God's standard. His standard is perfection, and no one is perfect. Because God is holy and just, He must punish sin. Just one sin during our entire lifetime is enough to keep us out of heaven. "For whoever keeps the whole law but fails in one point has become accountable for all of it" (Jas. 2:10).

Because He is holy and just, our sin has hurt, angered, and offended God and separated us from Him. "But your iniquities have made a separation between you and your God, and your sins have hidden his face from you so that he does not hear" (Isa. 59:2).

God's Word also tells us that the penalty for our sin is death. This separation is not only physical death but also spiritual death—separation from God forever. "For the wages of sin is death, but the free gift of God is eternal life in Christ Jesus our Lord" (Rom. 6:23).

All attempts that sinful people make to connect with a holy and just God (by their own effort) will always fail in reaching Him. God's standard is absolute perfection. No amount of our personal effort, good works, or religious deeds can earn us a relationship with God.

What are you trusting that you think will earn favor and approval with God? The church? Acts of service? Your background? Your parents? Your moral behavior? All attempts that sinful people make to connect with a holy and just God (by their own effort) will always fail in reaching Him. God's standard is absolute perfection. No amount of our personal effort, good works, or religious deeds can earn us a relationship with God.

God has provided the only way to give us an eternal relationship with Himself through the Lord Jesus Christ. Jesus said, "I am the way, and the truth, and the life. No one comes to the Father except through Me" (John 14:6).

Jesus is 100 percent God and 100 percent man. He is God the Son. Jesus proved that He is God the Son by living a sinless life, performing miracles, claiming to be God, and rising from the dead. "In the beginning was the Word, and the Word was with God, and the Word was God. ... The Word became flesh and dwelt among us" (John 1:1,14) "There is salvation in no one else, for there is no other name under heaven given among men by which we must be saved" (Acts 4:12).

Why did Jesus have to die to pay for our sins? Because God says that sin must be paid for by the death of a perfect (sinless) substitute (see Rom. 6:23; 2 Cor. 5:21).

Why is Jesus our only way to God? Because Jesus is the only one qualified to pay for our sins and die in our place on the cross. Three days after His death and burial, Jesus Christ rose from the grave, proving that God's promise of eternal life can be ours.

Jesus did what we could not. He made Himself the bridge between sinful people and a holy God. The only way you can be saved from the punishment of your sin in eternity and have a relationship with God that begins today is through Jesus who died in your place to pay the penalty for your sin.

What actions and characteristics of Jesus qualify Him to have first place in your life?

God's free gift of eternal life can be yours by putting your complete faith in Jesus Christ. In other words, believe He is the Person He claimed to be, the Son of God, and that He has the power to save you. "Everyone who calls on the name of the Lord will be saved" (Rom. 10:13).

Faith means trusting in Jesus Christ as the only One who can bring us into a right relationship with God. Faith means depending on Jesus and His substitutionary death on the cross to do for us what we could never do for ourselves. "Whoever believes in the Son has eternal life; whoever does not obey the Son shall not see life, but the wrath of God remains on him" (John 3:36).

This free gift can never be earned by doing good works. It is free to you, but it was costly to God, who gave His beloved Son. Jesus has already paid the penalty for your sin! "The free gift of God is eternal life in Christ Jesus our Lord" (Rom. 6:23). "For by grace you have been saved through faith. And this is not from your own doing; it is the gift of God, not a result of works, so that no one may boast" (Eph. 2:8-9).

You cannot give anything to God to earn salvation. You must give up your trust in your own efforts to please God and place your complete trust in Jesus' substitutionary death on the cross. You need to stop trusting in your own good works, attempts to obey or follow God, or your pride in thinking you are a good enough person to face God and instead rely 100 percent on what He did for you on the cross, where He suffered the punishment that you deserve to receive.

When you trust in Jesus alone as your substitute in dying (Jesus died for your sins in your place), God will then give you eternal life as a gift. To put it another way, He will save you with an everlasting salvation from sin, Satan, and hell without costing you a cent. It is hard to believe, it's so amazing, but God's gift of salvation is absolutely free!

The choice is yours. What will you chose? Will you place your faith in Christ and His death alone to save you? God is speaking to you right now through His Word. Pray this simple prayer now to receive the offer of eternal life in Christ.

God, I admit that I am a sinner. I believe that Jesus is Your Son and that He died to pay the penalty for my sins on the cross. Jesus, I now put my complete trust in You to save me by Your death on the cross. Thank you for forgiving my sins and giving me free eternal life. Help me to follow You and teach me to understand and obey Your Word. Thank you, Jesus. In Your name I pray this. Amen.

One point has come across loud and clear this week: rebellion is serious. The truth we've looked at has been the kind that should be encased with the label, "In case of emergency, break glass." If you feel in any way that this applies to you (and I think it does for all of us), break the glass and deal with the emergency. I echo Hebrews 3:12-15. If you hear the Spirit's voice, don't harden your heart as in the rebellion. (We looked at Korah's rebellion on day 2.) Why is it such a big, urgent deal? Because you don't know what tomorrow holds.

On Sunday night, October 8, 1871, D. L. Moody was preaching the gospel in downtown Chicago. He challenged the listening crowd to go home and "think about what I've said about the gospel and come back tomorrow and tell me what you've decided about following the Lord."

Sounds OK, right? "It's a big decision. Don't rush into it. Weigh your options." About the same hour that meeting was breaking up, a few blocks west of downtown, a blaze had begun in Patrick O'Leary's cow barn. By midnight the fire had jumped the Chicago River's south branch, and by 1:30 a.m., the entire business district (where Moody had been preaching) was in flames. By 3:00 a.m., the inferno had raced northward, jumped the main river, and devoured more than 100,000 homes. Not until after midnight the following day was the fire extinguished as a steady rain left Chicago smoldering and in rubbles with hundreds dead.

Many of the people who had heard the gospel on Sunday night perished in the flames. By not deciding to follow Jesus the moment they heard the invitation, they had missed their opportunity to respond to God's good news.

D. L. Moody's ministry was changed forever. He said, "From now on, every chance I get I will urge upon people a decision today to turn from their sin and leave it behind to follow God's Word. Today if you hear His voice, don't harden your heart." The writer of Hebrews repeats that warning three times (3:7; 3:15; 4:7).

It all comes down to this: when you hear God's Word, do something about it. Failure to heed with urgency is to continue in sin. How you deal with your sin defines you. No amount of spiritual desire can erase the effects of our rebelliousness until we deal with it God's way. Don't tolerate any secret sin in your life. Turn today. The longer it takes you to get back to God, the harder it will get. Some will read this and go on living as they always have. For certain, God will go after those people, but it will become increasingly painful for them to turn around. Every day of rebellion is another plank kicked out of the bridge back to God.

God often uses this in my own heart. If you want to go further with God than you have in years gone by, decide today that every time God shows you something, you're going to get after it. If He lays it out for you, don't put it off.

> What action or point of surrender has God been prompting you to make that you haven't acted on yet?

What are you waiting for?

Do you feel the weight of obedience right now in some area of your life? ☐ Yes ☐ No

Don't ignore His prompting. How quickly this life will end; how soon eternity will begin.

Rebellion Is Ultimately Against God

Make no mistake about it: rebellion is ultimately against God. God didn't see Korah's rebellion in the desert as against Moses. Numbers 16:11 says, "Therefore you and all your company are gathered together against the Lord" (NASB). That's the way it is with every point of rebellion. God takes it personally.

Is the Lord speaking to you right now about a rebellious attitude? Are you willing to consider that this word is for you today? Is this an appointment from God in your life? Pray that God will change your attitude.

What the Lord Is Teaching Me About Rebellion

1. Rebellion is a dangerous, deadly slope, especially with God.
2. God takes rebellion toward His ordained earthly authorities very seriously.
3. We are natural-born rebels all the way back to the garden of Eden.
4. Pride is the root of every sin, especially the sin of rebellion.
5. Refusing to bend to the Lord's training can lead you to an unrecoverable place with God.
6. You can turn today from your private rebellion and receive Jesus as your Savior.
7. The time to deal with personal rebellion issues is right now!

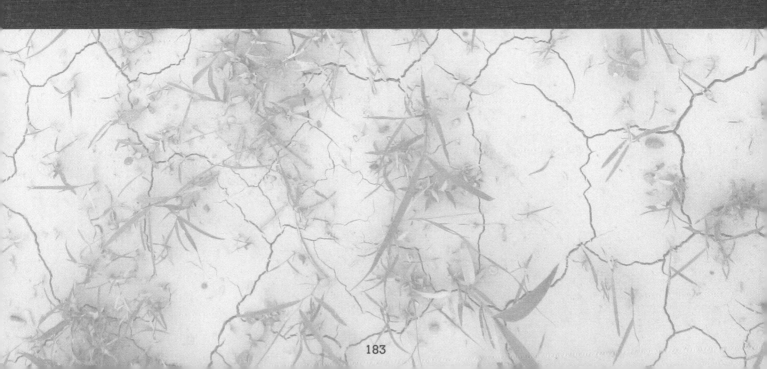

Week 10

WITH
SUBMISSION

Discuss in small groups. When have you experienced grace in your life? In what ways have you known the provisions of God in this way?

1. When did the children of Israel go too far?

2. What are the consequences of rebellion?

3. What are the steps leading to a shipwrecked life?

4. How are you doing in the study?

5. Why should people feel an urgency about changing this attitude?

Submission is for the
Lord's sake.
The law of God that you are rejecting.

Discussion Questions
About Rebellion

Video

Out of the desert at last, we've arrived at the attitude of submission. Watch, listen, and learn what the Bible says about submission and how you can have this attitude in your own life.

Video Notes

Submission is ~~favor~~ duty to God. Rom. 13:1   Ephesian 5:21

Submission—To operate within the established _authority_ ; to be under the chain of command that God has established. 1 Peter 2:13   1 Peter 3:1

Submission is _cooperation_ with God.

Submission is _protection_ by God.

Submission has _limits_ under God.

Submission is _voluntary_ , required by God but not to be <u>demanded by others</u>.   Acts 5:29

Submission is _favor_ from God.

Submission is _intimacy_ with God.

1. It depends on the source.
2. It depends on the severity.
3. It depends on the frequency.

Deut. 2:22

"Stand still and see the salvation of the Lord."

Discussion Questions
About Submission

1. How does submission relate to the other desirable attitudes?

2. Who should be submissive to whom?

3. Who is responsible for ensuring that someone is submissive?

4. How are submitting to God and submitting to people related?

5. How does submission affect your relationship with God?

Study Challenge

Submission may seem like a less desirable attitude than attitudes like faith or love. Pay close attention as you study this week to see why God wants you to have this attitude just as much as any of the promised-land attitudes we've already studied.

Memory Verse

"Giving thanks always and for everything to God the Father in the name of our Lord Jesus Christ, submitting to one another out of reverence for Christ."
Ephesians 5:20-21

Whatever! It sounds like I'm copping an attitude, but I'm not. *Whatever!* could be today's equivalent of a submissive response. When God's Word says to do something, a godly response would be to say, "Whatever You want, Lord." This kind of response is great evidence that your heart belongs to the Lord since we don't naturally submit to anyone. We are all natural-born rebels with a built-in resistance to submission.

Submission of any variety has a terrible reputation these days so it's hard to get even sincere people to consider it seriously. On top of that, biblical submission has been hijacked by selfish-minded, even cruel, authoritarians and twisted for their own purposes. The end result is that it's been unbiblically forced in a lot of situations.

I'm asking you to make a paradigm shift. Will you open your mind to the biblical concept of submission? If you do, you will see that when properly understood and applied, submission replaces the pain and strife of our natural rebellion and greatly increases our joy, peace, favor, and blessing from God.

Submission is not just for a few people. Contrary to what a lot of people think, submission is not just for women and children. Romans 13:1, NIV, makes clear that "everyone must submit himself to the governing authorities … which God has established." Everyone. It's for children just as much as it is for parents. It's for church members just as much as it is for pastors. It's for everyone. Ephesians 5:21 says, "Submit to one another out of reverence for Christ." Mutual submission is for both sexes and every age, social status, and employment relationship.

Put 1 Peter 2:13 in your own words.

What does the word "yourselves" imply about submission?

> Submit—a military term which means "to place yourself in order under established authority."

What does "for the Lord's sake" imply about submission?

Submission is a choice. It's not top down; it's bottom up. If you're in a role where you need to submit, that's a choice of heart God is asking you to make willingly. Husbands are not to demand that their wives submit. Pastors are not to demand that their people submit. A godly response to servant leadership is the choice of submission.

Blessing and favor come to the person who lives in submission. Why? God's will is "that by doing right you may silence the ignorance of foolish men" (1 Peter 2:15, NASB). Are you in a situation where you're being unfairly treated? Do right and silence the ignorance of foolish men. That word *silence* actually means "to muzzle." You say, "I know some people I would love to muzzle." Great! God's all for putting a muzzle on them, but you have to know how to get that done. It's by doing right, trusting God, waiting on Him, and living a life of biblical submission.

Why do you think it's so hard for people to receive the concept of submission?

Submission is like living under an umbrella. When we choose to submit, we put ourselves under God's protection. That's a wonderful place to live your life. Some bad things might be coming down, but submission is a covering. It's your place of protection. When you get out from under that, you become vulnerable. The promises of God do not extend to you when you choose to live as a rebel. However, when you choose to live under the umbrella of God's protection by submitting to His plans and doing what is right, all the promises and blessings of God are yours in abundance.

How does James 4:7 further illustrate this protection?

What do you do when things do not go the way "they should have"?

Peter's answer is this: "For this is the will of God, that by doing good you should put to silence the ignorance of foolish people" (1 Pet. 2:15).

Are you struggling with injustice? Have you been passed over for a promotion at work? It's not right, and it's so political. What should you do? Do right and silence the ignorance of foolish men.

Has someone turned against you in a relationship and injured you? Do right and silence the ignorance of foolish men.

Have you experienced a marriage breakdown and people think they understand what happened? Do you wonder how to defend yourself? Do what's right and silence the ignorance of foolish men.

Under Protection

A while back I was working in my office when my wife called me on the phone. She was frantic. Kathy's normally calm voice shook, "You have to come home right now. There's a bird in the house." We don't live far from the church, so I was there in a few minutes. Flying around our family room was a small bird, wild and crazed with fear. It was banging against the windows and flapping in a frenzy from one wall to the next. Feathers followed in its draft, and its cry was shrill and pathetic.

This bird's life was in greater danger the longer I took to capture it. That wasn't easy to do, however, because it was convinced that to let me hold it was the absolute worst thing that could happen. After maneuvering about for a few minutes, I held it safely in my hands. Only then could I feel it throbbing in terror. Little did it realize that secure in my hands it was better off than thrashing around the room. As quickly as I could, I got to the front door, launched the bird into the air, and it flew away.

Sometimes we feel like the worst thing that could happen to us is to be submissive to someone else's authority. The Bible often presents us with lines of authority that form boundaries around our lives. At first it's parental authority, school authority, government authority, a husband's authority, the church's authority—all ordained by God's ultimate authority. When we decide we don't want to be under the rightful authority, then we rebel and fly from this protection, banging into windows and walls, looking for escape. If we submit to God's Word, we fear we'll lose our autonomy or worse, our freedom—all the while killing ourselves in our frantic independence.

Need an Example?

I'm glad for the Bible's extreme practicality that gives wings to this truth. Take Ephesians 4:25-32 for example. This passage urges us to have convictions in one specific area: our speech. God promises His protection and freedom when we:

- Speak the truth (v. 25).
- Let no corrupting talk come out of our mouths (v. 29).
- Say only such as is good for building up (v. 29).
- Say only what fits the occasion (v. 29).
- Say only what will give grace to those who hear (v. 29).
- Put away all bitterness, wrath, anger, clamor, and slander (v. 31).

We could allow anything we think or feel to come flying out of our mouths, but to do so is to live in great jeopardy. How much better it is to rest in God's loving protective boundaries and be released to true freedom! Submission, when properly understood and applied, replaces the pain and strife of rebellion and greatly increases human happiness.

Case Study: Submission to God

She may have been in the middle of morning chores or perhaps escaping the noon heat in the family courtyard. Wherever Mary was, it was an ordinary day; and she was an ordinary girl dreaming about an ordinary future. Like every Jewish teenager, she had heard about the promised Messiah. Her parents and grandparents before them had discussed Isaiah's prophecy, longing each Passover for Messiah to come. Never had Mary considered the role God had planned for her to play.

We don't know what form Gabriel took when he came to Mary, but Luke 1:29 says that Mary was troubled by his words and what they meant. "Mary, you have found grace with God. You will bear His Son—the Messiah. God will do the impossible in your body!"

Humanly speaking, the entire course of Mary's life perched on her response. Her first question was *How?*—a question of logistics not faith. Her second response a moment later was complete submission to God. She said, "I am the Lord's servant. May it be to me as you have said" (Luke 1:38, NIV). Mary used the word *doulos* for "servant" meaning "a bondslave." A bondslave was committed to doing her master's will for her entire life. "May it be to me as you have said" was Mary's declaration of submission to God. The Greek word is *genoita*—loosely translated, "Whatever, Lord. Your will be done." Mary must have realized that this choice came with a price: doubts about her purity, whispers behind veiled glances, icy accusations: "Who did she say the father is?" But it was enough that God had entrusted her with this privilege. He was her Master; she would do what He asked. She would trust Him with the rest.

Every good step you've made in your spiritual life has been a step of humility. Isn't that right? Think about the seasons of growth you've experienced in your walk with Christ, those times when your faith went to the next level. Those seasons are marked by a sincere submission to God that opens our hearts to a genuine transformational encounter with the living Christ.

If you can point to a time when you came to Jesus for salvation, you know what humility is. On that day you said: "God, I need You. I need Your grace. I need Your forgiveness. I can do nothing to earn Your favor; I need what You are offering."

That's humility. You can't have a passionate, persevering relationship with Christ without it. You need to have the capacity first to submit yourself to God, then to submit yourself to the difficult circumstances of life to experience the full joy God intends for you to know. God often uses the painful circumstances of life to soften our hearts and to bring us to the point of brokenness to bow before Him. In those circumstances humility looks like this: "Lord, You're in control. You've allowed this for a reason. What do you want to teach me?" God loves moments when you're like, "Tell me what You are trying to teach me; I want to learn it. I want whatever You have for me." If you lack wisdom, ask. "I want to learn something new in this, God. I don't want to keep aching over the same hurts over and over! What is it, Lord?" That's humility, and in that place God will give you grace.

Humility stands empty-handed before God. No demands, no requests. In seasons like this, all we can do is fall into the embrace of our loving Savior and find Him to be enough. Humility says no to the clamoring voice of our flesh, no to the pride and self-confidence that has made us so restless and unhappy for so long. Every step forward is a step of humility.

Will you live a proud or a humble life? Hebrews 3 and 4 tell about how Jesus humbled Himself, how faithful He is. His model runs counter-culture to our world that wants to be on top—always best, always first. We want to stand out, but Jesus made Himself nothing. A day is coming when every knee will bow before the Lord, but in God's program humility comes before exaltation.

If it's true (and it is) that every step forward in your Christian life is a step of humility, then it's also true that every step of pride is a step backward. God help us to experience an overwhelming sense of our own personal sinfulness and to see rebellion against God for what it is and to bow our heads before God dozens of times every day if necessary. Through His strength alone, let's deal with this pride problem. If this is your desire, pray along with me.

Father, we humble ourselves before You. In bowing our heads and our hearts, we're saying that You are God and we are not. You are the Ruler; we are nothing. You are everything. Lord, we find great joy in that. How much misery in our lives has come from asserting ourselves and trying to prove ourselves? Forgive us for the lost opportunities to live for You because of our own pride. Strip us now of anything that promotes ourselves and fill us with Your Spirit.

May the example of Christ stir within us a fresh desire to live lives of humility.

A Word to Us All

The apostle Peter was on this same page when he wrote to the suffering Christians in the early church. If anyone had a right to rebel, it was these guys. "Likewise, you who are younger, be subject to the elders. Clothe yourselves, all of you, with humility toward one another, for 'God opposes the proud but gives grace to the humble'" (1 Pet. 5:5). This is a phenomenal truth: God is opposed to the proud. In this context the proud are those who are not submissive. He gives grace to the humble, those who will live under God's authority. At the end of the day, what really matters is the favor and the blessing of Almighty God.

More could be said on this matter. Issues could be explored and debated such as fairness and rightful disobedience. The final and best word should put all this to rest. The word is *Jesus*, seen through His friend's eyes, the disciple Peter. Peter, a witness to the greatest act of submission this universe has ever known, the cross of Calvary, said this about the Lord: "For to this you have been called, because Christ also suffered for you, leaving you an example, so that you might follow in his steps. ... When he was reviled, he did not revile in return; when he suffered, he did not threaten, but continued entrusting himself to him who judges justly. He himself bore our sins in his body on the tree, that we might die to sin and live to righteousness. By his wounds you have been healed. For you were straying like sheep, but have now returned to the Shepherd and Overseer of your souls" (1 Pet. 2:21,23-25).

In Jesus' power we can humbly submit ourselves to any authority, continuing to entrust ourselves to Him, Almighty God, who judges justly.

Lord, there are enough selfish, sinful people in positions of responsibility today to stifle anyone's joy. But Lord, my eyes are on You. You watch and know each step I take. I choose by faith to walk in obedience to Your Word. Help me to put off pride and put on humility in the midst of hardship. Help me keep my eyes on You and on You alone. Help me to wait and rest and live in obedience to You. Give me new strength to live in submission to You. In Jesus' name, amen.

What the Lord Is Teaching Me About Submission:

1. If you're in a role where you need to submit, that's a choice of heart God is asking you to make.
2. We are to submit to human institutions for our protection and for the process of getting God's work accomplished.
3. Submission to authority is like living under an umbrella.
4. Every step forward in the Christian life is a step of humility; every step of pride is a step backward.
5. The cross is the greatest act of submission in the universe, when Jesus submitted to God the Father's plan.

We're finishing our lesson on submission a few days early to give you a chance to put your attitude of submission into practice. On the following pages you'll find a tool for you to review and to reinforce what you've learned in this study. For the rest of the week, take some time for each page, intentionally thinking about and recording what the Lord has been teaching you on these 10 attitudes. Recommit yourself to apply each one as you go back over the lessons. Ask the Lord to show you something in review that you didn't see the first time.

Review Week 1, "Replace a Complaining Attitude ..."

Summary. Complaining is an attitude that if left unchecked will wither my capacity to experience joy and genuine thankfulness.

Spend some time praying about your complaining attitude. Ask God to help you see how it insults God and blocks the flow of gratitude in your life. Ask God to bring to the surface one or more statements or Scriptures that He wants you to understand, learn, or practice.

What was the most meaningful statement or Scripture to you in this lesson on complaining?

What does God specifically want you to do in response to this study on complaining?

Review Week 2, "With a Thankful Attitude"

Summary. Thankfulness is an attitude that perfectly displaces my sinful tendency to complain and thereby releases joy and blessing into my life.

Spend some time praying about developing a thankful attitude. Ask God to help you increase your awareness of all that He's done for you and to open your mouth to proclaim how grateful you are to be His child. Pray and ask God to bring to the surface one or more statements or Scriptures that He wants you to understand, learn, or practice.

What was the most meaningful statement or Scripture to you in this lesson on thankfulness?

What does God specifically want you to do in response to this study on thankfulness?

Review Week 3, "Replace a Covetous Attitude ..."

Summary. Covetousness, rampant in the Western world and the evangelical church, blocks the flow of God's fullness in our lives.

Spend some time praying about your covetous attitude. Ask God to show you what unfulfilled need in your life should be satisfied in Him. Pray and ask God to bring to the surface one or more statements or Scriptures that He wants you to understand, learn, or practice.

What was the most meaningful statement or Scripture to you in this lesson on covetousness?

What does God specifically want you to do in response to this study on covetousness?

Review Week 4, "With Contentment"

Summary. A consistent attitude of contentment can bring lasting joy and lead you out of the wilderness of covetousness.

Spend some time praying about developing a thankful attitude. Ask God to help you increase your awareness of all that He's done for you and to open your mouth to proclaim how grateful you are to be His child. Pray and ask God to bring to the surface one or more statements or Scriptures that He wants you to understand, learn, or practice.

What was the most meaningful statement or Scripture to you in this lesson on contentment?

What does God specifically want you to do in response to this study on contentment?

Review Week 5, "Replace a Critical Attitude ..."

Summary. A continuously critical attitude toward those around me will consume all that is healthy and joy producing in my life.

Spend some time praying about your critical attitude. Ask God to help you see how destructive and prideful this attitude is toward others. Pray and ask God to bring to the surface one or more statements or Scriptures that He wants you to understand, learn, or practice.

> What was the most meaningful statement or Scripture to you in this lesson on a critical spirit?

> What does God specifically want you to do in response to this study on a critical attitude?

Review Week 6, "With Love"

Summary. The only attitude big enough to replace a critical attitude is an attitude of love.

Spend some time praying about developing a loving attitude. Ask God to establish the "you before me" mind-set and so model Jesus Christ's attitude. Pray and ask God to bring to the surface one or more statements or Scriptures that He wants you to understand, learn, or practice.

> What was the most meaningful statement or Scripture to you in this lesson on love?

> What does God specifically want you to do in response to this study on love?

Review Week 7, "Replace a Doubting Attitude ..."

Summary. Those who make doubting their lifestyle will spend their lifetimes in the wilderness.

Spend some time praying about your doubting attitude. Ask God to help you see how this attitude slaps away God's hand and undercuts your entire Christian life. Pray and ask God to bring to the surface one or more statements or Scriptures that He wants you to understand, learn, or practice.

What was the most meaningful statement or Scripture to you in this lesson on doubting?

What does God specifically want you to do in response to this study on doubting?

Review Week 8, "With Faith"

Summary. Only when faith replaces doubt in the life of a believer can the joy of knowing God become a reality.

Spend some time praying about developing an attitude of faith. Ask God to help you increase your faith by reviewing all that He's done and, based on His character, how He will fulfill His promises. Pray and ask God to bring to the surface one or more statements or Scriptures that He wants you to understand, learn, or practice.

What was the most meaningful statement or Scripture to you in this lesson on faith?

What does God specifically want you to do in response to this study on faith?

Replace a Rebellious Attitude ... with Submission

Review Week 9, "Replace a Rebellious Attitude ..."

Summary. Rebellion against proper authority reveals rejection of God's authority, which brings devastating consequences to our lives.

Spend some time praying about your rebellious attitude. Ask God to help you turn from pride and respond positively to whatever God asks of you. Pray and ask God to bring to the surface one or more statements or Scriptures that He wants you to understand, learn, or practice.

What was the most meaningful statement or passage of Scripture to you in this lesson on a rebellious attitude?

What does God specifically want you to do in response to this study on a rebellious attitude?

Review Week 10, "With Submission"

Summary. Submission, when properly understood and applied, replaces the pain and strife of rebellion and greatly increases human happiness.

Spend some time praying about developing a submissive attitude. Ask God to help you increase your willingness to put yourself under God-ordained authority and experience the blessing of God's favor. Pray and ask God to bring to the surface one or more statements or Scriptures that He wants you to understand, learn, or practice.

What was the most meaningful statement or Scripture to you in this lesson on submission?

What does God specifically want you to do in response to this study on submission?

How to Perservere

Most of us are great at beginnings. We've set a high bar for our attitudes in our study. We've asked God to change us in some specific ways, and today we're willing to do what He asks in order to get that job done.

But what do you do when the pressure is on? All kinds of people get up in the morning, put on their jogging suits, and start the race. But when the miles click past and the muscles start to fatigue and life isn't easy anymore, what do they do? What will you do when your life's circumstances unfold in seemingly negative ways and you point the finger and start to complain and criticize? What will you do with contentment when the cash flow seems to flow in only one direction—out? How will you respond when God asks you to do something that you find completely unreasonable?

When you're under pressure, promised-land attitudes will be a frustrating distant memory. The truth is that no one can consistently live like that. And God never expected that you could. He knows that the Christian life done His way is done only in the power of His Spirit. What does that mean to you today?

Get your hands together and cup them like you're holding water. Envision holding all of the promised-land attitudes there: gratitude, contentment, love, faith, submission. Offer them up to the Lord with a prayer something like this.

You've said in Your Word, Lord, that these attitudes honor You and bless me. I've experienced them enough now to know I want these to be my natural response to life's challenges. I also know I've failed when I've tried to live this way in my own strength. All my good intentions amount to nothing but frustration. But now I have new understanding. I believe that You would never require something that You don't provide the ability to do. In the strength of Your Spirit, Lord, please live Your life in me. Be the focus of my thankful attitude. Be the fulfillment of my contentment. Be the object of my faith and the strong and trustworthy Master of my humbled heart. Fill me with Your power as I surrender myself afresh to Your sovereign, gracious hand today. By faith I say thank You for changing my attitude. Please keep changing me every day of my life until I see You face-to-face.

Name

Date

Epilogue

LORD,
HEAL ME

In small groups, discuss: Which wilderness attitude has convicted you the most? Which promised-land attitude has encouraged you the most? What is your goal as a result of this study?

1. How does God-ordained authority protect those who put themselves under it?

2. Why is humility important when you submit?

3. What is pride's role in relation to submission?

4. Who is an example in your life of humility and submission?

5. To whom are you willing to submit?

Discussion Questions
About Submission

Video

We've reached the end of our study. Listen and see what healing words you hear from James MacDonald and from the Scriptures he uses in this, his final word to you in this study.

Video Notes

Attitudes are patterns of thinking formed over a __long__ period of time.

The __circumstances__ of life bring us continually to a fork in the road.

Murmuring is __choosing__ the road that leads to the wilderness. *Number 21:5*

1. __Attitude__ reveals the true person. *Attitude* *(Its not what you eat; it whats eat at you)*

2. Attitude predicts the __future__

3. Attitude is __vertical__.

Repentance from murmuring is access to God's provision for _Victory_.

God's provision begins with people's _repentance_

God does not remove the _serpents_

The people had to _look_.

Hebrew 6:9
John 3:2-3; 7
3:14
Romans 5:8

Hymn
Look and Live

Discussion Questions
About "Lord, Heal Me"

1. How are your attitudes and your Christian life connected?

2. Who in the Bible, other than Jesus, is your greatest role model for promised-land living?

3. What do people have to do to improve their attitudes?

4. What often happens in difficult circumstances?

5. How can you have the victory in promised-land attitudes and living?

Study Challenge

Keep spending time in God's Word so your attitudes will keep you out of the wilderness and in promised-land living!

LEADER GUIDE

The following pages will help you prepare for and conduct an 11-session, small-group study of *Lord, Change My Atttude*.

Understand Your Role as Leader

You do not have to be a content expert to lead this Bible study. Your role is to facilitate each session. James MacDonald will provide inspiring messages from God's Word each week in a DVD segment. During the week participants will study this workbook and complete the interactive learning activities and prayer experiences. Through these content segments and learning experiences, participants will be ready to discuss the messages and share personal insights and experiences during group sessions. The two-page spread at the beginning of each week's lessons provides a practical guide for your small group session. On those pages you will find:

- a small-group ice breaker discussion question, often related to the previous week
- small-group discussion questions about the previous week's home study
- an introduction to the video
- a fill-in-the-blank listening guide for the video
- discussion questions about the video
- a challenge for the coming week's study

In many cases, following the suggestions for each of these segments, together with prayer times, will fill your small-group session. If you have more time, you may choose to use some of the additional suggestions on the pages that follow. By using these resources, you can be a lead learner along with the other group participants. You could even share leadership with another small-group member if desired or necessary.

Pray

The verb in the title of this study is *change*, and change is rarely easy. Because attitudes are formed over a long period of time, participants may not at first recognize that their attitudes need to change. Or they may want to change but have difficulty changing. Pray that God will draw participants into the study and make them open to His direction in their lives. Pray that they will respond to the Lord in repentance and willingness to change.

Set a Time and Place

This small-group session can take place at any time that is convenient for participants. Sundays, weekdays, or Saturdays will work, daytime or evening. We recommend 90-minute sessions so that you will have adequate time to view the DVD segments and process what God has taught and done during the week. Plan for plenty of time for members to share and to pray together.

Groups may meet at the church building, in homes or apartments, in a community meeting room, in a workplace before or after work or over lunch, in a school, or almost anyplace. The availability of a television or projector and a DVD player, sufficient space, and enough privacy to prevent interruption are the primary factors that may limit your choice of locations.

Determine Fees

Each participant will need a member book for the small-group study. Determine the cost for each participant so that you can mention it when you advertise the course. Usually people are more faithful to use the member book and to attend group sessions when they have made a personal investment in the resource. Be prepared to provide partial or complete scholarships when needed so that no one will be excluded from the study because of financial considerations.

Set the Group Size

The best small-group dynamics take place in groups of 8 to 15 members that remain consistent over time (in this case 11 sesions). Smaller groups may be too intimate for some but are satisfactory if members know and trust one another. Larger groups are too big to allow everyone to participate. If you have more than 15 participants, consider dividing into multiple groups. If your church has multiple groups meeting at the same time at church, you may choose to watch the DVD messages as a large group and divide into small groups for content discussion and response to the DVD message segments. If you use this format, consider keeping people in the same small groups each week. Don't require people to get acquainted and develop new relationships each week. They need to develop trust for sharing deeper thoughts and feelings as the study progresses.

Enlist Participants

Use your church's normal promotion channels to advertise this study: bulletins, posters, newsletters, PowerPoint® slides or video before the service, announcements, Web site, and so forth. The DVDs include a promotional segment that will introduce the study and invite participation. This study is appropriate for both believers and nonbelievers. The study moves toward an opportunity for nonbelievers to accept Christ in the last week.

Order Resources

Each participant will need a member book (item 005035039). Because each person will need to give individual responses to the learning activities, a married couple will need to have two workbooks instead of sharing one copy. You will also need one leader kit (item 005097385) for your small group. The kit includes one copy of this member book, one copy of the original book from Moody Publishers, and three DVDs with weekly sessions, an interview, and a promotional segment. The DVD sessions have a weekly teaching segment from James MacDonald.

To order resources, write to LifeWay Church Resources Customer Service; One LifeWay Plaza; Nashville, TN 27234-0113; e-mail *orderentry@ lifeway.com*; fax (615) 251-5933; phone toll free (800) 458-2772; order online at *www.lifeway.com*; or visit a LifeWay Christian Store.

Secure Equipment and Supplies

Secure the following equipment and supplies for use during the sessions.
- ☐ Television or projector and DVD player
- ☐ Name tags and markers
- ☐ Whiteboard and markers
- ☐ Roster for keeping attendance records if desired

Preview the Course

You may prefer to study the entire member book and view all DVD messages before beginning the study with your small group. However, you may study one week ahead of your group and have a good experience. Before the first session view session 1 on the DVD and study week 1. Be prepared to explain that members will use this book to complete five daily lessons each week and will participate in weekly small-group sessions.

Be Ready to Introduce James

Read "About the Author" on page 4 and be prepared to introduce James MacDonald to your group at the first session. To find out more about his ministries, go to:
- *www.harvestbible.org*
- *www.walkintheword.com*
- *www.lifeway.com/jamesmacdonald*

The last site describes products and events by James MacDonald offered by LifeWay Christian Resources.

Prepare for Each Session

1. Pray for the members of your group during the week. Be sensitive to the Holy Spirit's prompting about calling, e-mailing, or sending a note of encouragement during the week.
2. Study the content for the week.
3. Preview James MacDonald's DVD message for the upcoming session.
4. Review the session plans that follow for each week as well as the activities described on the introductory pages at the beginning of each week's study. Determine which activities and questions will be best for use with your group.

Decide on a flexible time schedule for the session so that you have time for each segment of the session.

5. Secure a television or projector, a DVD player, and the DVDs from the leader kit. Make sure the equipment works.

6. If members do not know one another well, provide names tags so they can get better acquainted with other members.

7. Provide a chalkboard, whiteboard, or flip chart and chalk or markers. Provide extra Bibles for participants.

Session 1
Replace a Complaining Attitude ...

1. As participants arrive, greet members and ask them to make a name tag and to write on a sheet of paper at the registration desk their name and other information as indicated (phone number, e-mail address, address) to help you stay in touch during this study.

2. Distribute books and collect fees, if any.

3. Pray for this study and for members' lives to be changed.

4. Invite members to turn to pages 6-7. Guide the group through the first group activity.

5. Introduce James MacDonald using the author information on page 4.

6. In small groups talk about the four discussion questions on page 6.

7. Encourage members to complete the video notes as they watch the first DVD segment.

8. Watch the video.

9. In small groups discuss the video content using the questions on page 7.

10. Explain the use of the workbook and encourage members to complete the study for week 1 prior to your next session.

11. Close the session with the study challenge and with prayer.

Session 2
With a Thankful Attitude

In addition to the group process outline and suggestions on pages 32-33, consider the following ideas:

1. Ask a member to quote the memory verse for week 1 (Phil. 2:14-15). Encourage members to memorize the key verses each week.

2. Discuss sarcasm. Ask a volunteer to read Exodus 14:11-14. MacDonald says this is sarcasm. Have you recognized sarcasm in the Bible before? How are sarcasm and complaining similar or different? Have you heard sarcasm this week? In light of this week's study, what did you think when you heard it?

3. Ask these questions about a complaining attitude: What do you think about the idea that ordinary, everyday complaining is an insult to God? Why do you think this is true/not true? If it is true, what should we do about it?

Session 3
Replace a Covetous Attitude ...

In addition to the group process outline and suggestions on pages 52-53, consider the following ideas:

1. Ask a member to recite the memory verse for week 2 (1 Thess. 5:18).

2. Ask if their outlook during the week was better as they focused on thankfulness rather than complaining. Ask volunteers to share some experiences of how their awareness of what they and others say has been heightened during the past two weeks.

3. In preparation for the study on covetousness, invite someone who works for a bank or in a financial role to present a few statistics about debt and bankruptcy in the U.S.

Session 4
With Contentment

In addition to the group process outline and suggestions on pages 70-71, consider the following ideas:

1. Ask a member to repeat the memory verse for week 3 (Matt. 6:20-21).

2. Ask: What evidence do you see that the covetousness is a significant concern in the U.S. today?

3. In preparation for next week's study on the attitude of contentment, ask: Is being content with what you have a good idea? Why or why

not? How does being content with what you have differ from being content with who you are? Where do you draw the line in being content with who you are and striving to improve?

Replace a Critical Attitude ...

In addition to the group process outline and suggestions on pages 88-89, consider the following ideas:

1. Ask a member to repeat or read the memory verse for week 4 (1 Tim. 6:6-10).
2. Ask: What temptations have you faced this week in the area of money and possessions? Were you content or covetous? What have you decided about the desirability of being content? How can you be content and continue to want to grow and improve at the same time?
3. Before you begin reading about a critical attitude, what do you think most people criticize? Do you think some people have a critical spirit and approach everything that way? When, if ever, is criticism a good approach?

Session 6
With Love

In addition to the group process outline and suggestions on pages 106-7, consider the following ideas:

1. Ask a volunteer to recite or read the memory verse for week 5 (Eph. 4:29-32).
2. As you review your study about a critical attitude, ask: What is the difference between criticism and analytical thinking? Share any ideas you've created to stop yourself from coming out with complaining or critical comments.
3. In preparation for this week's study on love, ask: Do you think love is the opposite of a critical attitude? Why or why not?

Session 7
Replace a Doubting Attitude ...

In addition to the group process outline and suggestions on pages 126-27, consider the following ideas:

1. Ask a participant to recite the memory verse for week 6 (1 John 4:10-11).
2. As you reflect on the promised-land attitude of love, ask: Do the previous attitude checks help you move toward an attitude of love? Why or why not? Does self-understanding and acceptance make it easier to love others? Why or why not? What kinds of things block having a loving attitude for many people?
3. In preparation for the week's study on an attitude of doubt, in advance, invite someone who has experienced a crisis of doubt to share a brief testimony about what it was like and how he or she overcame it or kept it under control.

Session 8
With Faith

In addition to the group process outline and suggestions on pages 144-45, consider the following ideas:

1. Ask a member to recite the memory verse for week 7 (Jas. 1:6).
2. As you review an attitude of doubt, ask: How can Christians help one another when someone is dealing with doubt?
3. In preparation for your study on faith, enlist a senior adult to tell about how his or her faith has endured through tough times as well as good times.

Session 9
Replace a Rebellious Attitude ...

In addition to the group process outline and suggestions on pages 164-65, consider the following ideas:

1. Ask a participant to repeat the memory verse for week 8 (Heb. 11:1).
2. As you reflect on your study of faith, ask: What advice would you give a new Christian about cultivating an attitude of faith? How are faith and hope alike or different?
3. In preparation for the study of rebellion, play Frank Sinatra singing "My Way" and discuss why it is an appropriate anthem for an attitude of rebellion.

Session 10
With Submission

In addition to the group process outline and suggestions on pages 184-85, consider the following ideas:

1. Ask a volunteer to recite the memory verse for week 9 (Prov. 16:25).

2. From your study on a rebellious attitude, ask: Is all rebellion against God? Why or why not? Is there ever anything good about rebellion? If so, what? Is linking pride to rebellion legitimate or not? Why?

3. In preparation for the study on submission, enlist a woman to affirm submission, or enlist two people to have a brief debate on submission.

Session 11
Epilogue: Lord, Heal Me

In addition to the group process outline and suggestions on pages 198-99, consider the following ideas:

1. Ask someone to recall the memory verse for week 10 (Eph. 5:20-21).

2. The title of the epilogue is "Lord, Heal Me." Ask participants how they feel at this point having closely examined their attitudes. Do they need healing? In what way? Does healing mean going back to the way they were before encountering this study? If not, what's next?

3. Ask volunteers to share some personal goals as a result of this study.

Two Ways to Earn Credit
for Studying LifeWay Christian Resources Material

CHRISTIAN GROWTH STUDY PLAN

CONTACT INFORMATION:
Christian Growth Study Plan
One LifeWay Plaza, MSN 117
Nashville, TN 37234
CGSP info line 1-800-968-5519
www.lifeway.com/CGSP
To order resources 1-800-485-2772

Christian Growth Study Plan resources are available for course credit for personal growth and church leadership training.

Courses are designed as plans for personal spiritual growth and for training current and future church leaders. To receive credit, complete the book, material, or activity. Respond to the learning activities or attend group sessions, when applicable, and show your work to your pastor, staff member, or church leader. Then go to *www.lifeway.com/CGSP,* or call the toll-free number for instructions for receiving credit and your certificate of completion.

For information about studies in the Christian Growth Study Plan, refer to the current catalog online at the CGSP Web address. This program and certificate are free LifeWay services to you.

Need a CEU?

CONTACT INFORMATION.
CEU Coordinator
One LifeWay Plaza, MSN 150
Nashville, TN 37234
Info line 1-800-968-5519
www.lifeway.com/CEU

Receive Continuing Education Units (CEUs) when you complete group Bible studies by your favorite LifeWay authors.

Some studies are approved by the Association of Christian Schools International (ACSI) for CEU credits. Do you need to renew your Christian school teaching certificate? Gather a group of teachers or neighbors and complete one of the approved studies. Then go to *www.lifeway.com/CEU* to submit a request form or to find a list of ACSI-approved LifeWay studies and conferences. Book studies must be completed in a group setting. Online courses approved for ACSI credit are also noted on the course list. The administrative cost of each CEU certificate is only $10 per course.

LifeWay
Biblical Solutions for Life

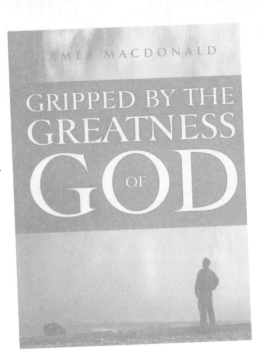